THE CORONA
SILVER LININGS
ANTHOLOGY

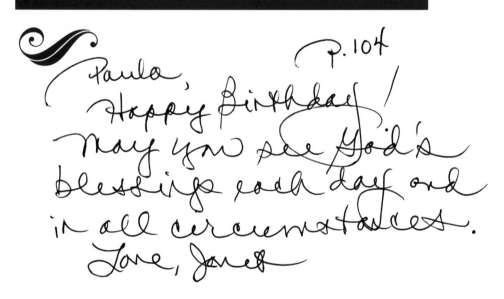

Paula,   p. 104
Happy Birthday!
May you see God's
blessings each day and
in all circumstances.
Love, Janet

LifeWrite Press

ISBN 978-1-49-583090-7 Paperback
ISBN 978-1-49-583091-4 Hardcover

Published December 2020

Lifewrite Press
517 Boston Post Road, Unit 593
Sudbury, MA 01776
www.lifewrite.org
info@lifewrite.org

This book is dedicated to the memory of all those who lost their lives from Covid-19, and to the First Responders who dedicate their lives to saving ours.

Prologue

We are living in a historic time. We mourn for the lives that have been lost. We empathize with all those in pain and suffering in their physical or mental health, the lack of financial stability, and the drastic shifts in their lives. We recognize how difficult this has been on the youth throughout the world who have had to adapt their way of learning, socializing and celebrating milestones. We know that they will never get another Senior year of high school or college, another Prom or graduation, or the multitude of experiences they have all missed.

And yet, through all the tragedy and challenge, we know there is more. We know that if we dig deep enough and search within ourselves and our situations, we can find the life lessons, the acts of kindness, the situations which highlighted our inner strength and resilience and the silver linings that emerged from the darkness. Highlighting these aspects while creating a thought-capsule of this global pandemic, was the impetus in creating *The Corona Silver Linings Anthology*.

At LifeWrite we believe that everyone has a story to share, and our goal is to help share it with the world. These pieces prove that. You will hear a 13-year-old's viewpoint alongside that of an 85-year-old. You will read words and stories from well-established, published authors to those whose submission was their very first attempt at sharing their writing with others. But each piece will touch you, in a unique way, for each individual's story taps into universal truths and connects us a little more closely. Words from the heart enter the heart. And these pieces will most definitely do that.

Not only was this project an opportunity for people to share their experiences, but in doing so, it helped others as well. LifeWrite is the non-profit initiative of Opyrus.com, and each submission came with a donation to our partnering charities: The First Responders Children's Foundation and First Book. The proceeds from the sales of this book will likewise help Covid initiatives.

So, thank you for reading *The Corona Silver Linings Anthology*. We have no doubt it will resonate for you in many ways. And we hope that as you read these silver linings, you will likewise find your own, and feel inspired to write your own story, as the world needs to hear it.

I would like to take this opportunity to thank the people that made this publication possible. First and foremost is Arthur Gutch, CEO of Opyrus. It was his vision, passion and dedication–from inception to production–that gave this book the professionalism it deserved. His insight, support and direction were invaluable.

The backing and support of Jorian Polis Schutz allowed this dream to become a reality and we are so grateful for his commitment to sharing positivity and connectivity through the written word.

And Bruce Butterfield, a senior advisor to Opyrus, and The LifeWrite Project, whose expertise and help with this project was immeasurable.

I am grateful to the Opyrus team for their help throughout: Gabe Chavarria for his excellent work in design and composition, Christian Shelton for his digital marketing prowess, and Daniel Spyralatos for his social media and growth hacking expertise. Thank you to Rishe Groner for her careful eye in copyediting, Tzudi Couzens for his help in reviewing and reading all submissions, Patrick Fore for his powerful photograph used for the cover, and Tri Widyatmaka for his cover design.

This was truly a group effort in every sense of the word, and I am honored to have been able to manage this project and bring to you *The Corona Silver Linings Anthology*.

Enjoy!

Sara Esther Crispe
Executive Director
The LifeWrite Project

Table of Contents

QUARANTINE & ISOLATION: 67

ACTS OF KINDNESS 131

Sickness, Loss; Healing & Health 209

PARENTING & FAMILY

LINDSEY WARDEN

LOCKDOWN, NIGHT AND DAY

My toddler's newest refrain echoes through our small two-bedroom home every night at bedtime without fail.

"Hold hand, hold hand!"

While he used to be a beautiful sleeper, giving up breastfeeding at thirteen months and generally sleeping in his own little crib all night without fail from that point on, ever since we began living in isolation in our historic Memphis, Tennessee neighborhood, his nighttime wake-ups became nighttime anxiety, and he can barely let a parent out of his sight in the evening without melting down into sobs that wrack his slight frame, tears puddling on the collar of his pajamas.

He's too young to understand why his daycare shut down, or why visits to Granny and G-Pa are suddenly fewer and farther between. He doesn't see why I, his mother, a veteran teacher by trade, logs off from one more Zoom class and lays my head on my desk in utter defeat, nerves frazzled from a day spent on screen with middle schoolers, who would in all likelihood be better off outside, playing in the sunshine. He can't comprehend the terseness of his father, my husband, whose employer shut down as the pandemic reached its height, making him suddenly our son's primary caregiver during the day and our resident bill-payer by night. Long after we have finally gotten our child to sleep, my husband hunches at our dining room table, poring over mail from collectors and loan sharks, trying to figure out how we're going to make ends meet with a sixty percent reduction in our income.

Daytime is fine. We cook all of our favorites. I make savory waffles in the morning with perfectly poached eggs on top, delighting in the silky yolk breaking on my plate, reminding myself I would never have time to poach an egg during my regular busy workweek. My husband experiments with baking bread and desserts, true to the lockdown stereotype, and we eat our fill of banana nut muffins, double chocolate brownies, peanut butter cookies, and berry cobblers. I splurge despite our financial straits and fill our backyard with a slide, a swing, a sandbox. COVID-19, its effects, and even its method of spreading were still very much unknown in the earliest days and I reason that we might as well enjoy our backyard as a family while we still can.

We avoid the news, and religiously wipe down groceries and takeout boxes with Lysol wipes before touching them. By the time our Lysol wipes run out and are nowhere to be found on grocery store shelves, we have already learned that the virus is mostly spread through respiratory droplets. Our canned goods and fried rice containers are safe. I stalk Amazon for bulk diapers and order them whenever I can get my hands on them, knowing they will be bought up within hours. I live with a toothache for two weeks, terrified to go to the dentist and potentially expose myself to the virus.

We walk. Around and around our block each evening, we walk. They start with a circle around our neighborhood and back. Then we start walking two miles, then three, then five, then to our favorite restaurants, where we cautiously eat on the patio, leaving quickly if anyone sits down near us. We walk in the nearest park, and then we walk in a new park, and another and another until we find our favorite one, twenty minutes outside of the city, with a trail next to an idyllic creek, densely wooded, shady, and cool.

As we walk, we talk more than our busy lives as employees and graduate students had afforded us before. In our ten years together, we talk more during this pandemic than ever before, laughing at the antics of our son, admiring his golden curls, fretting over the health of our parents, debating the presidential election. My husband catches my hand as our son toddles on ahead, joyfully hitting a stick against every tree.

"You're beautiful," he says, and I smile up at him, wiping sweat from my forehead. My first years as a teacher followed by graduate school and a pregnancy were not kind to my body, and now as the world locks down, I find every opportunity to get outside and move.

When our son sleeps late in the mornings, or plays quietly with his wooden trains and tracks, we find moments to lay in bed together, lazily loving, instead of occasional, frantic encounters snuck in somewhere between a graduate seminar and potty training. I feel young again, although the pandemic also makes me feel very, very old.

Daytime is fine. Sometimes, it is even joyful, peaceful. Sometimes it is right. But at nighttime, our laughter-filled days spent in isolation are pierced by our son's howling cries from his bed, demanding.

"Sit here," he dictates in a high-pitched whine, patting the bed next to him. "Sit here. Hold hand."

And we do. At night, as I curl into my two-year-old's bed and pull my heirloom quilt over his warm, tired body, his stuffed orangutan, his juice cup, I keep his own dark fears at bay as well as my own. I imagine forming a protective cocoon around us, his father, our cats, our house; that the world cannot penetrate with all of its destruction. I trace his little features as his drowsy eyes close and he drifts easily into sleep, assured that his mother is near and all is well, and I know I'd give anything to push this mother's soothing power outside of my four walls and into all the world, until we can each rest easy, the hurts and fears of the day put to bed.

Lindsey Warden is a teacher and mother from Thompson's Station, Tennessee. She has lived all over the South, and enjoys spending time with her family, cooking vegetarian meals, studying genealogy, and reading anything she can get her hands on.

Lindsey Warden's son

BROOKE KAELA DIAMOND

MOVEMENT OF TIME

Life was a beautiful monotony, until a single shard broke it.
What seemed like seconds now appears to be much longer
A solitary moment expands while we wait for it to end,
Leaving me to wonder, as I race forward, how much longer until
    time advances

I can sprint no longer, for I must catch my breath.
And then I realize I'm not alone.
A sea of masks surrounds me,
And I feel clustered and cramped, despite everyone being
    distanced.

For weeks, I don't move forward.
The light emitting from my electronic device is a comfort,
as this precious object keeps me connected to humanity.
At this point, I'm not sure if I know how to walk anymore.

Some people thrive in the disorder
They strive forward while others remain frozen in time.
It makes me feel like I'm wasting away, and I should be doing
    something.
What have I done to use this experience for the better?

It comes more naturally to others to speak out about what we
    should do
what we haven't done and what we did wrong.
It's easy to lash out at others from behind a screen
It's easy to miss the mask that covers your heart.

Many people decide to be left behind.
They reassure themselves that it's okay to hide,
to bask in your misery like a drug.
There's such a thing as too much validation.

There comes a point when you can't just lie in bed any longer.
no matter how warm those covers are that protect you from this
    gruesome reality.
The more I think about the future, the harder it is for me to
    accept this.
I'm like a little kid asking their parents how much longer the car
    ride is.

I understand the desire to let yourself drown in desolation
It's effortless to tell others to pick themselves up, but harder to
    do it yourself.
It's simple to let the quicksand absorb your body and soul
But much harder to push against the unsteady ground and
    continue to move forward.

I know I can't continue like this.
So I pick myself up, dust off my pants, and start to walk.
My legs move faster, and soon I am flying, soaring to an
    unknown goal
Friends and family run with me, 6 feet away, but they don't feel
    far.

I hold onto the things I do have, the people who do exist.
Adaptation has never been my strong suit, but I must adapt.
I must change.
The world I live in is changing, and I can't be left behind in the
    past.
I need to keep going.

I'm a 15-year-old high school student who enjoys reading and writing. I hope for my work to express myself, and help others know that during this time of turmoil, we can find solace in literature, especially pieces that let you know you're not alone.

16

RIDLEY PEARSON

LOVE IN THE TIME OF **COVID**

Our family merged at the Denver airport. It was the middle of March 2020, and our home state, Idaho, was heading into full lockdown. We changed various flights five times to arrange a family reunion—our daughters live together in NYC—so we could drive the three hours from the airport to our home with the least risk of virus infection. We might have been scared. We were certainly cautious. We'd never faced anything like this.

We were greeted the next day by moose eating our massive weeping willow tree, dating back to the early 1900s. With snow still on the ground, the moose had found our home and its magnificent tree. We live in the middle of a very small town. They had stepped over our picket fence to reach the tree. We took pictures. We laughed at our new friends. They would return another few times, but with us living there, and our dog, they soon moved on.

That was how quarantine started.

Three out of four of us were working online eight to ten hours a day. We established footholds in our small home, declaring our office spaces. I ended up—no kidding—at the back of a walk-in closet, where I'd used carpentry clamps to attach an old piece of plywood to a shelf that had once held my socks. The plywood became my desk. I wrote there for months, wedged between my outdoor sweatshirts and my dress shirts. My view was of a basket of white socks and my underwear.

We arrived to the fourth highest infection-rate-per-capita in the entire country. Our little valley that supports a major ski resort was in the thick of the COVID-19 onslaught. I became the grocery shopper and cook, taking extreme measures to protect the family. We sheltered in place for three months, only going for short walks or hikes well away from others after that.

And we fell in love again.

My wife and I hadn't lived with the girls since their high school years. Now Mr. 19 had handed us the chance to be together day and night for five months and one week. Our daughters moved back to NYC four days ago. We miss them horribly. But the laughter at dinner, the fun in the kitchen, the re-watching of Disney movies, the sharing of personal tragedy, the church-over-Internet, brought us so much closer. Closer than ever. It is like our family is somehow starting over again; we know each other in ways that would never have been possible had we not sheltered away from this ongoing horror.

In the past two weeks four friends and/or family have died. Not COVID related deaths, but age, disease and freak tragedy. My shared office partner was infected and survived Mr. 19. We trudge on with heavy hearts. It's not over yet, nor does it appear it will be for a very long time.

But through it all, we found love. We are the lucky ones. The video calls with our daughters bring bittersweet reunions. They have no idea, we think, how sorely they are missed. But their lives start over. Ours go on. And the days begin to drag out once more.

NY Times best-selling and multi-talented author, Ridley Pearson, has written over 50 novels - the popular Kingdom Keepers series, *over two dozen crime novels (including* Probable Cause, Beyond Recognition, The Risk Agent*), and the Tony Award-winning* Peter and the StarCatcher. *He also plays in "The Rockbottom Remainders" rock band along with Stephen King, Scott Turow, and Dave Barry.*

MARIANNE PEEL

Do Not Be Afraid to Open Your Windows and Sing

Tonight I listened
to the quarantined people of Sienna, Italy
sing out their windows
into the dark of the night,
trusting that the sound of their sole voice
would connect
to someone who needed that melody.
And the old woman hanging her towels
on the balcony
caught that tune
let if float down onto her scrubbed
and sanitized hands
and instead of balling her fingers into a fist
she opened her palms
placed them on the balcony ledge
added a harmony line
just two intervals below the melody
and floated it into the vibrating Italian air.

The pregnant woman
watering the bougainvillea on her balcony
caressed the roundness of her belly,
felt that determined beating heart

and then opened her lips,
adding a soprano obligato
above he notes coalescing
on this street overflowing
with open windows,
with hearts that long for connection.

We shine our best
in the darkness.

DISCOVERY IN THE TIME OF CORONAVIRUS

Until tonight
I thought I had touched
everywhere on you.

But now
in this time of
no need to set the alarm
in this time
where you are
the only person I touch
I discover a small soft patch
on the underside of your upper arm
a vulnerable place
new to me.
Unexplored territory
on the geography of you.

And suddenly
we are making love
as if for the very first time
in a dorm room in Istanbul

accompanied by Turkish seduction music
and a jangling belly wrap
sensuous surrounding my hips.

> I remember the hijabed woman
> who sold me the wrap
> in the marketplace,
> knowing my hips would welcome
> intimacy that very night.
> She nodded and winked at me.

And tonight
I want to touch her hands
transfer my gratitude to her fingers
eleven years later
for her silent knowing.

Love in the time of Coronavirus.
Tenderness in my hands.

SMALL GESTURES

It's the little things
    Making sure there is a jar of Lysol wipes in every car
    at every door entrance
    even using one jar as a doorstop

    Offering to fetch vanilla creamer for me at the Piggly
     Wiggly
    sugared clouds for my coffee
    after waking at 3am

    Wiping down the door handles

until your palms are raw
and you smell of sterilized sanitation

Washing your hands before you hold mine
asking *Are you ok?* And when I nod, unable to make eye
  contact,
you ask *Are you sure?*

You remind me
I haven't been sick in almost seven years,
even though meds designed to blunt
my entire immune system are pulsing in my blood
doing their work.

You remind me
that even at Kara Tepe Refugee Camp,
a village filled with coughs and rashes
and people seeking asylum,
even there
where I welcomed refugees to the camp clothing store
holding their feet in my hands hoping for an acceptable fit
  of shoes,
even there
my lungs did not succumb.

You remind me
Love over fear.

But at night
when I try to close my eyes,
I see us on a bed
floating in the dark, adrift.
We are the sweet old couple

from the Titanic
suspended in a determined embrace
floating unmoored
to the sounds of the tenacious string quartet on deck
making music without hesitation
long after we have fallen asleep
in each other's arms.

QUARANTINE DAY 15

When my mind won't settle in for the night
we play this game:
Tell me three good things,
I implore my lover.

I took a good shower, he tells me.
And then silence.

I didn't have a meltdown today, I tell him.

Tomorrow I will make a Spanish stew.
We shall serve it up in miniature bowls
and call it Tapas.

There are still sticky notes
yellow and pink
scattered around the apartment.
His outreach gesture
to help me learn Spanish.
Most have lost their adhesive
and have fallen to the floor.
The label on my toothbrush
has dissolved into the bottom of the glass.

The letters are water-logged.

I am incapable of memorizing anything now.

The words on these Spanish love notes
blurred now
and utterly indecipherable.

FINDING LIFE IN THE GRAVEYARD: DAY 45 OF QUARANTINE

Weaving our way through the scrub sanctuary
our feet take on the sand
and the ash
of a deliberate burn.

Our steps shrouded
in the most fragile of silences.
Whole trees lay prone on the ground
hollowed out from the proscribed flames.

The fires burned here
unevenly, indiscriminate
of wings or bud
of bloom or leaf.

And if we listen with places our ears
cannot hear,
green tendrils now sing
from the knotholes.

A wordless lyric

accompanied by scrub jays and a southerly wind.
Palm leaves lattice themselves
with pine needles, precarious on charred branches.

There is no limit
to this resurgence of living vines
in this graveyard place.

And if we listen with places our ears cannot hear,
we absorb this sanctuary cadenza
open-throated and leaning into the light, echoing
reborn,
    reborn,
        reborn.

Marianne Peel is a retired English teacher, and after 32 years nurturing her middle/senior high students, she is now nurturing her own voice. Marianne has a book of poetry forthcoming from Shadelandhouse Modern Press in Spring 2021.

JENNIFER HENEHAN

PERMITTED

When school let out in mid-March 2020, we still had plans. We planned on a spring break trip to Hawaii. We planned on travelling all over the west coast for sailing regattas. We tentatively planned to go to Italy in the summer for a regatta. My son planned on two weeks away at the YMCA summer camp. But in the annals of what really matters to teenagers, my 15-year-old daughter planned on getting her driver's permit on April 8.

Her California Department of Motor Vehicles (DMV) appointment was scheduled in January. All she could think about was getting her permit. In California, permits are available when the 'driver' turns 15 and a half. Since her birthday is September 30, her half birthday is March 30. As no appointments were available that day, we had taken the earliest available: April 8.

The DMV closed shortly after schools closed. Thus, began the daily litany of questions about when life would get back to "normal" so she could get her permit. In the face of a global pandemic, with stay-at-home orders, limitations on the packages of meat one could buy at Costco, and shortages of pasta at Trader Joes, the truly important issue was "WHEN WILL I GET TO TAKE MY PERMIT TEST?"

We endured April at home. The days were filled with haphazard Zoom lessons and some efforts at homework. Nights were board games and another home-cooked meal (aka experimental food). Some afternoons were 'art' lessons with Bob Ross and his wonderful YouTube channel. We have several oil paint canvas masterpieces that adorn the laundry room, courtesy of Bob Ross and his happy little trees. Throughout all of this, "WHEN WILL I GET TO TAKE MY PERMIT TEST?"

May was interminable. The days blended together, and we often forgot what day it was altogether. We slept, ate, played games, and kept moving forward. She kept asking the big question, "WHEN WILL I GET TO TAKE MY PERMIT TEST?"

Finally, at the end of May, the DMV opened for essential business only. Try explaining to a 15-year-old girl that her permit is not on the list of essential services provided by the DMV. We went to one DMV to see if it would be worth trying. There were several hundred people in a line that wrapped around the block, waiting to get in. The first people had arrived in line prior to 4 am – that is four hours before the DMV would even open its doors.

On June 13, after hearing that more offices were open, and that they were allowing permit tests, we tried again at a smaller field office. Because we had all of our paperwork ready, we were able to submit everything online and skip to the 'appointment' line, even though we didn't have an appointment. One hour after arriving at the DMV, she had her permit. She will be able to take her in-car driver's test on December 14, six months and one day from the date of her permit. For her, the tough year that has been 2020 will end in success, if she is able to pass her test that day.

She has been driving for two months now. Life will never be the same. Just the other day, she drove to Costco and we made it in and out of the parking lot unscathed, though pulling in and out of parking spaces takes years off of my life.

She has now gone through a huge checklist of firsts:

Pumped gas – check.
Mom yelled at her while driving – check
Dad yelled at her while driving – check
Passengers gasped while driving – check
Drove the front tire into the curb – check
Scraped the hubcap and knocked it off the rim – check
Picked up fallen hubcap off the street – check
Replaced the hubcap on a wheel – check
Parents doubting the wisdom of her driving? – check

At this point, I am a mother, trying to keep the household and the teenagers sane enough to make it through the global pandemic. If we can all make it through understanding that uncertainty is a given, and not a cause for panic, then life is good.

LUCERO DE ALVA

A Silver Lining in the Lives of Migrant Children

For the last few years, the influx of migrants into the US from Central American countries has been on the rise.

Fleeing extreme poverty and violence, these children arrive at the US/Mexico border, without knowing what to expect.

So, to create a sense of normality during this pandemic, I began working with them on a daily basis, providing education, physical activity, art and entertainment.

It has been challenging since in this shelter, I just get to work with them during their quarantine, after that, they are sent to other shelters that, along with the state government of Chihuahua, have been supporting migrants since 2018. Here, it is a motel where each family lives in a room that they cannot leave for any reason, unless it is the outside front part of it. This makes things way more complicated, since I have to stand outside, and with all my love – and the help of a microphone, speaker, printed activities, jumping-ropes, seeds, soil, crayons, pots, notebooks and scissors, all provided by my friends from SEGUIMOS ADELANTE -I reach out to not only their ears, but also their hearts and souls.

With only little time to plant all the seeds that I want to leave in their soul's soil, I thought it was going to be very difficult. Which was great, because, what is more challenging than having to adapt to their needs instead of just doing the usual stuff? In my case, I have always been a volunteer and an advocate for children. I don't care what part of the world they come from; for me, the children of the world are our children, and we are in big debt toward them, I personally believe this, so, with or without material resources or enough time, I will always work something out, no matter the place or the situation that these little ones are facing at the time I decide to support them.

When it comes to education, I don't mind if they will only get to spend 14 days with me. In fact, even if it was only one day, I'd do my best to make it count, so that means a bit of mathematics, geography, grammar and history are always a part of our daily academic activities. I have seen Mateo (eighty years old) and Ashley (nine years old) having so much fun just learning how to use a compass. I have also seen the challenge that represented for Wilson (twelve years old) and Naomi (eleven years old) just trying to remember the multiplication tables; but I have to say that comprehension reading activities and science experiments are, above all, their favorite. I loved watching Diego (eight years old) trying to think of adjectives to describe the 'giant' after I read them *Gulliver's Travels*, and David (nine years old) taking so much care of the sunflower that he just transplanted from a glass jar, to a pot, after watching the germination process of the seed that he first covered in cotton and then watered on a daily basis.

I have also witnessed how yoga and meditation classes have brightened their days, and how jumping rope and throwing water balloons at each other from afar, have always provoked a big smile on them...SMILE, what a beautiful word when it becomes part of their daily lives.

I have also seen how the practice of art has helped them bring out their emotions; either while creating the scenography for the 'Cinderella' theatrical play, or watching Liliana - a thirteen-year-old girl from Guanajuato, Mexico, who arrived to this city after her mom was killed - representing one of the step-sisters character. Watching her having so much fun with her dress and her make up on, made me cry so much because I felt that I contributed at least a little to disconnect her from her cruel reality.

Maybe some people could say that all of these efforts are useless, but for me and my friends, bringing a big screen, popcorn and ice cream, so that for the first time in their lives, they could experience what going to the movies was, and then listening to their screams when the giant dinosaur was running after Tim and Lex in *Jurassic Park* - was just PRICELESS.

During difficult times, such as this pandemic, it is 'us', the volunteers, who have the busiest days. The more things there are to do; little and big sacrifices become part of our routine, as we try to find the time in our already busy schedules to commit to these children. Volunteering, for me, has always been something that I take very seriously. It's not just something I do when I have some free time, or when all my basic needs are covered.

As a mother of four amazing children that are now adults, I have experienced an uncountable amount of silver linings in our lives. I feel extremely grateful every time one of my daughters or my son, refers to their childhood as a magical and beautiful experience. So why not do something so every child in the world can say the same? I know it is not an easy thing to accomplish, but it is also not impossible. The wonderful thing about children is that you can make them happy with so little. If your love for them is authentic, they will, for sure, love you in return - and what is greater or more powerful than love?

My only hope is that one day -,I don't care when - at least one of them will remember this pandemic as a 'fun and meaningful' part of their lives, knowing that a 49-year-old woman, in outside temperatures of 112' F, went outside that motel and poured her heart and soul over their lives, during these difficult, challenging, but unforgettable days.

I am a 49-year-old woman, entrepreneur, teacher, mother, writer and volunteer. I have spent the last three years of my life working with children, bringing seeds of peace to their schools. Since February 13, 2018, I also began volunteering with migrant children that are looking for asylum in the USA but have to wait here during their process.

MICHELE DIAMOND

GOING FORWARD

On September 11th, 2001, I was in downtown New York. Like many others, I carry with me the painful memories and images of that day. It saddened me to see the loss and devastation to those close by, while I was also grateful for being safe. I was incredibly touched by how that experience brought people together, and had tremendous admiration for those who risked their lives to help others. That event had a profound impact on me, and on how I moved forward in my life. It prompted me to learn many valuable tools and strategies for managing life's challenges, and to appreciate much more the value and joys of life.

When COVID hit the world as we knew it, it brought up my memories of 9/11 - but this time, of far greater magnitude. I found myself confronted once again with those intense feelings of grief, and at the same time, gratitude that my family and I were safe. My kids were born after 9/11, so to them, it was a part of history that I was in, far removed from their world and reality. I was concerned about how my kids would get through, remember, and reflect upon this major event when they grow older. In my ideal world, I envisioned the four of us (my husband, my two teenage daughters, and myself) using our time at home as an opportunity to elevate our personal and spiritual growth.

On this mission, I immersed myself in tons of online classes and workshops for information and inspiration. By observing and listening to what others were doing, I was motivated to do much of the same. However, despite all of the time, effort, and energy I put towards making our reality into what I saw and admired in other families, I found myself feeling frustrated, disappointed, and defeated. What I personally wanted for my family was not what they actually wanted. Having their goals conflict with mine challenged me to figure out my next option. I had to let go of my expectations, and instead focus on how I wanted to invest my time at home to create meaning and purpose.

As part of this plan, I took the time to evaluate who I was and where I was at this point in my life. I used this information to guide my plan going forward. The first step was to focus on priorities. Although I already knew the value of living life in priority order, and that time was a precious resource, COVID took this meaning to a whole new level. Getting older and also not knowing what lies ahead, I want to make sure that I make the best use of my time every day.

Many reoccurring lessons surfaced, as well as some new insights. I am so much more careful about how I choose to spend my time and other resources — knowing that every 'no' I make leaves room for a 'yes.' For me, this means saying no to finishing books that I once felt obligated to finish just because I started them. Now, I only read books that I really want to read. It means saying no to invitations I would have previously said yes to because I wanted to show support and not offend anyone. Instead, I now use that time for activities that I would regret not doing. Limiting news and interactions with negative people gives me more time and energy. Although I do not consider myself a materialistic person, before COVID I did enjoy my regular manicures, having a housekeeper, going to movies, dining in restaurants, and some personal indulgences. The only thing I am happy to have back is cleaning help. Learning to say no has allowed me to say yes to enjoying many of the simple pleasures in life, such as walking or hiking with my husband, cooking dinner with my family, watching movies together, and engaging in other fun activities. I also relish more time at home to read, take online classes, and build upon my spiritual practice.

I still think it is incredible how others from first responders, essential workers, the many volunteers, and all those out there (including families) shared their 'special something' with others to make their lives and the world a better place. Yet I needed to stop comparing my insides to another's outside. Each of our lives comes with its own unique and personal package for us to use on our life's journey. My job is to use what is inside my package to make a difference. It might not look like or be as big, brave, or impressive as others, but it might make one little change that could make a huge difference.

As for my family, I wanted them to join me on my spiritual journey, make the best use of their time, and look back on COVID as a catalyst for their own transformation. But just as I cannot compare myself to others, I cannot impose my goals on them. They will have a different experience of what COVID meant to them, yet it will be their own. Hopefully, the changes I have and continue to make for myself will positively impact them later on.

COVID has made my heart ache for all those lives lost and for the loved ones they left to grieve. I am also humbled by all the love, care, and devotion that has come forth in many different ways - a true testament to humanity's greatness! I hope and pray that our world is healed of COVID and all of its other ailments and that we all live together in good health and peace.

Being confronted with another catastrophe has also brought many blessings. My strengthened faith offers me comfort and guidance. I have found incredible support, encouragement, and resources by connecting to an online community. Clarifying my priorities enabled a closer relationship with my family. All these have transformed and elevated my day and life!

I enjoy sharing what I have learned in hopes that it can help another, and I also appreciate what others share that is helpful to me.

TOBY HECHT

QUARANTINE WEEK 11 - A LOOK BACK

My kids and I were eating dinner in Brooklyn one evening a while ago, pre-COVID, when two young men approached us. They asked me politely if my daughter, then eight, could help them with discerning a letter on a *mezuzah* scroll they were holding. According to the code of Jewish law, if a scribe is unsure of which letter is written on a sacred text, he can ask the opinion of a young child versed in the Hebrew alphabet. Every letter in a sacred text must be kosher; i.e. precise, exact, otherwise the entire text is invalid. This is referring to the *mezuzah* (placed on the doorpost), *tefillin* (phylacteries) and the Torah scroll – the most sacred of all Jewish texts. The child should be neither 'wise nor foolish'; the law says. Foolish not to know the difference, or wise enough to know the expectation. It can seem preposterous that a young child should determine the validity of a letter, and thus the entire body of such holy work, yet it is the case. A child, who is pure, is undeterred by personal opinion or agenda, and can just focus on the appearance, giving a clear unhindered answer. Valid or invalid.

I love this concept and seeing it with my daughter in real time made it unforgettable.

We were in week four of quarantine when this lesson reasserted itself, and took on new meaning for me.

I was exhausted. The first few weeks had felt like years, there was too much information to process. I couldn't fathom the idea of catching this terrifying illness, which was wreaking such havoc on a global scale. Everything and everyone had been thrown in flux with no end in sight. In the middle of the chaos and noise, I saw something compelling in the periphery of my vision. My kids, especially the younger ones, were jamming to their own rhythm. They weren't foolish or wise. They knew something was going down, and that it was important – but they weren't distracted by thoughts of impending doom. They found a clear channel to a new normal, and hopped on without a backward glance. Over the rainbow, so to speak.

So, I decided to take their lead as much as possible. I surrendered myself – my order, my schedule, my worries – for a time, and strapped to their backs I went with them over that rainbow. The dining room and office became the classroom and workspace with me as the class monitor. It was hard, and they did it anyway. We went on long bike rides and training wheels became two wheelers, young encouraging younger. Grassy parks became football fields and a perfect place to throw down an unused quilt to soak up the sun near a winding path or a racetrack. The annual renewal that spring delivers was sumptuous and gorgeous, the air crystalline and fresh.

Backyards transformed into paradise and competitive drill sites, a solitary tire swing became the mother of all rides. Overgrown shrubs became clever hideaways with welcome signs. Stories were spun under the shade; soft gesticulations of small hands stained with dirt. Dormant shadowed brush suddenly became prime hunting ground for accessory to the imagination. Loud choirs of celestial harmony filled our ears every day, a complex musical score; the birdsong. Normally drowned out by other sounds, their conversational melody flowed unencumbered as they waved in and out of the sky, a pattern; to tree to earth back to sky. Complicated puzzles became accepted familial entertainment giving our overstimulated brains an agile exercise, and our hearts a unique bond. And we learned and debated and argued and prayed and internalized as we celebrated *Shabbos* (the Jewish Sabbath) after *Shabbos*.

It was bittersweet – in its most genuine expression – utopian bubbles among burdensome fear, tangible gains amidst devastating loss. Lifelong lessons were condensed into moments. We felt sorrow and joy equally and often simultaneously.

History tells us that there is an indeterminate amount of insight and knowledge to gain from challenging times. Perhaps, with an uncertain future and the human spirit at risk, we can remember the words of Malachi the prophet in the Bible. "*Veheishiv lev avos al bonim v'lev bonim al avosom*" – "the hearts of parents will be inclined towards their children, and the hearts of children will be inclined towards their parents". Let us look to the children for clarity to inspire faith and courage, and in turn they will follow in the wisdom of our ways.

My name is Toby Hecht. I live in New Haven, CT with my family. I am one of the directors of Shabtai, located near campus at Yale University.

SEAN MOONEY

HOPE IN DISASTER

I'm a dad. Actually, I'm lots of things – a scientist, a writer, a teacher, a husband, a son, a brother, a friend, a counselor, a philosopher - but dad is how I've come to recognize myself. I'm also, by nature, a pragmatist – which is a fancy way of saying I'm a pessimist, but I'm not going to assume a good thing will lead to a bad thing. Usually. Sometimes. I enjoy the world and what it has to offer, but I don't find much hope in it. Maybe I am a pessimist?

I look at the world – a world of people who are willfully denying simple facts and truths, people who are deliberately being selfish, people who are so utterly self-absorbed by their desires that they can't find ways to keep themselves entertained at home for three weeks or wear a mask in order to put a chokehold on a virulent and deadly virus. I see angry people who won't take a moment and think about someone else. I see people who can't accept the difference between the physical and metaphysical world, fantasy and reality, want from need. I see people who cheer at earthquakes in California or a nightclub shooting, or gleefully assume that a deadly virus is an act of their god - sent to purge the wicked and reward the righteous. I see that these people are, by and large, a small percentage of the world, but often have the loudest voices and have the most significant impacts on society. I see a lot of things I don't like, and I am perfectly capable of knowing that A plus B will inexorably equal C.

I also see people protesting. Certain politicians – people who are in the greatest position to do the most good - who are trapped, as all good guys often are, by rules and ethics, so much so that at a cursory glance, it looks as if they aren't doing anything to help when in fact they've done all that they can in accordance with what they are allowed to do. I see responsible news organizations asking the hard questions, even if they tend to get distracted by shiny new stories and ratings. I see people who are trying to make a difference – and sometimes succeeding. I see whole nations coming together to battle for the greater good. I see people using their hate and love to do extraordinary acts of good. I see the world for what it could be.

And that vision, that glimpse of what the world could be – that is why I am foremost a dad, because even if I don't check social media, I see it at home every day. I accept dad as my main title because my son gives me hope of what the world could be. During this time, he has accepted with good grace being stuck home during his birthday. He has accepted, without teenage attitude, being distanced from his friends. He has accepted with pride that wearing a mask is what you do not only to help yourself but, more importantly, to help others. He has been comforting and strong when so many, just a few years older, have been narcissistic. He has cheered for protests, and he has tried to explain to the ignorant that helping someone, or asking for help, is in no way a sign of weakness. He has been wise enough to recognize that when anger has manifested in unhelpful ways, it is time to question why. The window has been smashed, but why is far more important than whom. Why can lead to change. Why leads to knowledge. Asking why gives you an answer – if you're willing to listen. My son has been a beacon of hope not only through this pandemic but as a vision of what this country, this world, could be – will be.

The artist Michelangelo, when asked about how he made his sculptures so lifelike, said that he did very little. The statue was already there; he simply carved away the unnecessary pieces. I feel as if the world is what actually carves the beautiful sculpture of my son. It chips away the unnecessary pieces and my wife and I are simply the safe studio where it happens. The pandemic, the ugly responses, and the protests for sanity, for equality, for accountability that have bubbled to the surface during this time, have all molded him, and those like him, into champions. Champions, I hope – I know – who will take this disaster and make sure something good comes from it.

I'm a scientist, turned stay-at-home-dad, turned writer - who also helps run a homeschool group.

KIM FLUXGOLD

HONOUR THY GRAD

From the moment the lockdown orders went into effect here in Ontario, Canada in mid-March it very quickly became apparent that my youngest daughter's senior year of high school was not going to look quite like the one she had been dreaming of since first entering high school some four years earlier.

Things began to unravel pretty fast for her and the millions of other students around the world who were eagerly approaching their graduation day. It started for us here at home with the sudden cancellation of a once-in-a-lifetime high school graduation trip just two days before our daughter was set to leave to Punta Cana with her friends, when the government of Canada strongly advised all Canadians that any and all non-essential travel be halted immediately. This was just the beginning of a long list of further disappointments to come as the virus' force began spreading feverishly around the world.

So when the inevitable was finally announced a month later in mid-April, that her prom had been officially cancelled and that her graduation ceremony was to be postponed indefinitely, my heart broke even further for her. That was when I knew that I needed to do something to help honor so many deserving graduates – and not just the high school ones, but all graduates needed to be recognized for their efforts, starting from PRE-K to postgraduate education.

Everything these kids had worked toward was being taken away from them; their rites of passage included. I came up with the idea of making lawn signs to honor them in some small way. I created six different unique slogans for parents and loved ones to choose from. I knew that I also wanted to give back and help those who had been suffering the most throughout the Pandemic; our young people. I decided to donate all of the proceeds from my initiative to Kids Help Phone, as I felt as though they were made for a pandemic. They are a charitable organization which provides free and confidential 24/7 help to all youth in Canada via phone, text and online services, meaning that any child in need of support can get it, without ever having to leave their home.

I also knew that Kids Help Phone could definitely use as much extra support as possible during this time, as their services were in greater demand than ever. Just thinking about how many of our young people around the globe were dealing with so much raw and uncertain emotions from this pandemic made me want to ensure that they have as much access as needed to get the help they deserve. And whether they are feeling anger, sadness or frustration, Kids Help Phone is a safe place that allows young people to feel less alone or afraid. Many more of our young people have also been feeling very anxious, disappointed and depressed since the pandemic began, which are all very natural feelings to have, and perfectly valid and understandable given the current state of the world, having to be forced to quarantine away from friends and family, and away from all the activities and social events that they love and miss so greatly.

I myself have been suffering with major treatment-resistant depression as well as severe anxiety for six years now. From my own battle with mental illness I have become a mental health advocate, which I write about on my blog, 'YouAreEnough.' Talking openly about my own journey has helped grow many positive conversations toward ending the stigma surrounding mental illness. I also wrote a children's book titled *"Where Did Mommy's Smile Go?"* which aims to teach parents and caregivers how to help children cope with and understand their feelings when someone they love is suffering from depression. These two feats are what helped me push through to the very end of my six-week campaign this past spring. It was very overwhelming for me, but I made a commitment to our youth. I was not about to give up until every single sign I sold was delivered and installed proudly on a very deserving graduate's front lawn.

My simple idea to honor some graduates grew to 700 signs being hand delivered by my husband and I within the greater Toronto/Hamilton area of Ontario and a donation of $10,000 to Kids Help Phone. The outpouring of support and kindness that I received from both Graduates and their loved ones truly made this the most rewarding success ever.

Kim Fluxgold is a children's book author, blogger and mental health advocate. She lives in Concord, Ontario with her three beautiful children, her precious puppy and her amazing husband.

Signs made by Kim Fluxgold

JEANINNE ESCALLIER KATO

❧

THE IDOLS OF MARCH

March 2020, was the last month of my visits to the elementary and middle schools where I coached beginning teachers for the state of California. We knew COVID-19 was coming, but districts hadn't yet received the governor's edict for school closures. When I entered both campuses the week before schools closed, I could have cut the anxiety with a butter knife. It was palpable; everyone felt it.

I air-kissed my teachers and eagerly accepted a healthy dose of hand sanitizer when I left each classroom. We dedicated our hourly visits, normally set aside for observations and teaching techniques, on ways to weather the impending storm of this deadly virus. Watching the children run and jump on the playground filled me with dread. I knew something ominous was approaching from which those unsuspecting, joyful children couldn't be sheltered.

I lived for my students' joy for thirty-six years. I couldn't imagine worrying about national school closures before the last trimester of each of those sacred years, nor could I imagine a parent's fear in the face of a world-wide pandemic. Like the day Japan attacked Pearl Harbor, our lives would be forever changed.

I couldn't have my own children, but I learned to be a parent from each one of my students. When California schools closed in mid-March, my first thoughts were: *What about all those seniors who can't attend their proms, who can't walk the stage in front of their families to get their diplomas, who can't have their all-night parties, marking their transition from adolescence to adulthood?* I felt like a parent whose daughter or son had just lost the best part of twelve, dedicated school years. My heart shattered into tiny pieces of unfulfilled dreams.

I also thought about my transition from adolescent to adult. The day of my high school graduation is as clear to me now as it was forty-eight years ago. Before real life hit - supporting my own college education, travelling the world, surviving a failed marriage and learning I couldn't have biological children, enduring my father's death, enjoying a successful marriage, publishing a book, and retiring after thirty-six years of teaching - I was a naïve young woman who believed in happy endings. That graduation day was a culmination of everything to which I aspired since the day I broke free of my mother's hand on my first day of kindergarten.

I dashed out of the house in my hip-hugger jeans that graduation morning with a Pop Tart in one hand, my pink minidress with bell sleeves rolled up in the other. My mother yelled, "Jeaninne, take out your juice can rollers!" I kissed my Mary-Tyler-Moore-look-alike mother in appreciation. Once my hair was board-straight with the middle part, I jogged one block to my high school campus. My drama friends met me in the auditorium to rehearse snippets of our best plays to present at the Baccalaureate assembly for the entire student body.

After rushing around to say good-bye to the teachers who inspired me to teach, I slipped into my pink dress and reapplied my black mascara and frosted peach lipstick. The whole school was ushered into the auditorium. Before the principal introduced the entertainment section of the assembly, where I would recreate my roles as Mary in *The Women* and Mrs. Kellar in *The Miracle Worker*, awards were given to deserving seniors. I was one of the ten Senior Girls of the Year for my extracurricular accomplishments and high academic standing. I had gorged on everything about the high school experience like a starving man in front of a royal buffet. It was my time to shine.

After the assembly, we seniors were allowed to roam the campus to get our yearbooks signed and to collect our navy blue cap and gown. I puffed up with pride when the registrar said, "Jeaninne Escallier, your gold braids and gold tassel are at the next table." I had earned the right to wear the California Scholarship Federation symbols of academic success for four years as a straight-A student.

Minutes after the last bell, I banged in through the back door of my tiny house with one bathroom and yelled, "Everyone clear the decks, I have to get ready to graduate!" Pictures of me on the front lawn in my cap and gown with my mother, stepfather, brother and stepsisters are faded now, but that day is still crisp and vibrant in my mind. (My mother even snapped a photo of me in my underwear, while I wrestled into my long halter dress that had to be taped up under the gown.) I was bursting with unabashed energy to celebrate with my friends.

In our alphabetical lines, we walked out to the football field and took our seats on the metal folding chairs. I looked around at my classmates, those adorable children I had known since kindergarten, as the sun set behind the stadium. An overwhelming surge of love and pride weakened me at the knees. I squeezed Junior Escamilla and Baltazar Esparza's hands when I heard my name. As I walked proudly across the lawn, Kent Fillmore, the smartest boy in our class who had graduated a year early, yelled out from the stands, "Yay Jeaninne!" I waved my diploma, blowing kisses to my family.

I met my friends in front of one of many buses waiting in the school parking lot to take five hundred giddy seniors to the all-night party at Disneyland. I hugged my friends tightly and said, "I will never forget this day or any of you, ever." I never have.

I'm thinking of all those hopeful seniors now who have lost out on these important milestones because of COVID-19. However, I'm certain they will be the generation that leads America through future disasters with even more strength and fortitude. Congratulations Class of 2020! America will never forget you.

Jeaninne Escallier Kato is a retired educator and current education coach. She is the author of the children's book **Manuel's Murals.** *Jeaninne finds her muse in the Mexican culture and dedicates her vast literary work to the thousands of California students who have given her wings.*

LOVE YOUR NEIGHBOR

Even the smallest acts of thoughtfulness, make a difference.

Stay well,

Astrid Sheckels

Award-winning children's picture book author/illustrator, Astrid Sheckels, is beloved by many. She is a multiple winner of The Moonbeam Award (Nic and Nelly, The Fish House Door) *and her classic,* The Scallop Christmas *was a Lupine Honor Award winner.* Hector Fox and the Giant Quest *is another family fun fan favorite. She has published with Random House, Islandport Press, and Twin Lights.*

Astrid Sheckels Art

KAT MCKANN

LIBERTY ACRES AND THE TERRIBLE SCARE

On Liberty Acres Farm all was well.
Winter was ending the critters could tell.

They were joyous with the coming of spring
and for the wonderful things spring would bring.

Then, one day, a hush fell over the land;
a strange silence they could not understand.

No one knew why there was no one in sight
or why the family had tucked in tight.

So Vi, the chickadee, said she'd fly out
to learn what was happening all about

and come back, quick as she could, with the scoop
so they all could be kept in the news loop.

Waiting anxiously for the news they'd get,
they all hummed, as the sun began to set.

When, at last, Vi returned she didn't feel well
but perched on a limb and began to tell.

She gave her report with a sad-toned song
and, to their dismay, they learned before long

that a dreadful dust, blowing through the air,
was covering everything everywhere.

It was a horrid thing, this dust, it was
and this dust scared everyone just because

they hadn't seen anything like this before
and so, that scared everyone even more.

Some folks were caring for ones who fell sick
while others were trying to find the right fix.

When Vi was done they knew what they should do.
They would have to get, safely, tucked in too.

Libby Lou Ladybug flew to her nest.
Moe Mouse scurried back home, as it seemed best.

Tate Cat and Jax Dog stayed on the front porch
but could still chat with others back and forth.

Clancy Pig and Grady Goat kept from harm
by sheltering up, safely, in the barn.

Katie Cow and Rosie Horse joined them there.
To keep themselves and others safe, was fair.

Staying put was I, Mighty Mama Oak,
with my little acorns tucked in my cloak.

Baby Nut Nuts, and his squirrel kin there too,
caring for Vi, who seemed to have the flu.

Then, through the stillness, came sounds from afar
uniting, in song, under a bright star.

Together, by the light of the full moon,
they made a wish for all to be right soon.

We are not sure what the next day will bring.
In the meantime, let's continue to sing.

Sing praises for the workers everywhere
sacrificing so much because they care.

Sing praises to neighbors, strangers and friends
with their show of love a breaking heart mends.

Sing praises to families holding strong.
Home is our heart's beat and where we belong.

Sing praises to all trying to keep us calm
while giving advice to keep us from harm.

Sing songs together of faith, hope and love.
Make a wish upon a bright star above.

We're all in this together,
that is true
and with faith, hope and love
we'll make it through.

*Kat McMann, a poet, published children's author and songwriter, was
raised on a farm in Kennebunk, Maine and has always had a passion for
educating and inspiring kids of all ages.*

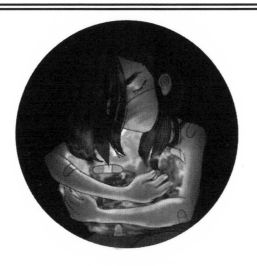

*We dedicate this to
the frontline workers and first responders
for their courage and dedication
during the
Coronavirus pandemic.*

- Kat & Zoe -

DORIT SASSON

NOTES FROM AN IMPERFECT LIFE

1) It is possible to think that the show I'm in right now is just a temporary displacement for uncertainty. And yet, this is where this show begins after months of dialoguing around doubts and fears as our summer getaway inches closer. How safe will we be?

2) Notes from an imperfect life: We are sitting at a picnic table at Presque Isle State Park in Erie, Pennsylvania. My six-year-old daughter has just lost another front tooth. Her white shirt is stained with blood. I wonder if I'll get the blood out before we head back to our Airbnb. Right now, there's nothing else to do but observe the puffy grey clouds, the geese and their antics, the surreys passing us by right and left. We dip baby carrots in hummus. I crave rice cakes and a nice hot cup of tea after our big biking adventure to warm up my insides.

3) Notes from an imperfect life: An hour before, my daughter and I biked through an ecological preserve on a tandem. It was the first time I'd ridden a tandem. It was clunky and vibrated, but it was gloriously free. After we had stopped to observe some birds, my daughter asked, "How do you spell freedom?" I spelled the word slowly, pausing between each letter. How did I suddenly become more loving and patient with this feisty, energetic kid after months of quarantine?

4) Notes from an imperfect life: The swamps and lagoons are breathtakingly beautiful, but she doesn't have the

patience to appreciate nature's candy like me, so we start heading back to the bike rental office where her father is waiting. I'm lost in deep reverie. When we enter a pocket of heat that wafts, then cools, I drink in memories of sleepaway camp and freedom. These rare moments give respite during these incredible times.

5) Up we go on the tandem and once again, notes from an imperfect life: the chain rattles and suddenly, it falls altogether. I brake and call the office. Within minutes, a breathless young man brings another tandem and when we return the bike, I receive two free bike passes. I silently yip all the way. Another sign of divine providence. Later that day, I'll bike in the other direction, but this time, with her fifteen-year-old brother who doesn't have patience for tandems. At least we'll create memories together. At least he'll get to taste freedom after months of not seeing his friends and his grandparents. This is how our family nest egg gets richer.

6) Notes from an imperfect life: While we munch on baby carrots and wait for the bleeding to stop, my husband stands up. He's been eyeing the father of a family who has gotten physically close, much less than six feet and now stares at us with his beaky nose and beady eyes because of our conversational Hebrew. Like the rest of the family members, he's wearing a *kippa* (skullcap) and *tzitzit* (fringes worn on garment) - a rare sight in this neck of the woods. Clearly this moment binds us together, but all of us are trapped in this beautiful fragmented Diasporic world that leaves me ruptured and pained. I sense that image of awkwardness and silence will haunt me for days to come. But we are safe here. In this moment.

Dorit Sasson is the award-winning author of Sand and Steel: A Memoir of Longing and Finding Home *(Mascot Books, 2021) and* Accidental Soldier: A Memoir of Service and Sacrifice in the Israel Defense Forces. *She provides SEO services as a copywriter and strategist.*

MARGARET KOVICK

FINDING THE WAY HOME

Someone once told me, "you will never appreciate your parents until you're alone and sick and there's no one to take care of you."

At the time, I was eighteen, reckless, and full of false confidence. *I do appreciate my parents*, I had thought. Months later, traveling across the US, I came down with a case of strep throat that left me holed up in my tent for two weeks, unable to speak and barely able to eat. Still, I didn't fully appreciate the sentiment. "Young people bounce back"; was another mantra I had heard, and I liked that one more. So, I bounced back to my new young adult freedom, and didn't dwell on thoughts of my parents.

Years later, in my small Roman apartment, the phrase drifted back to me: *You will never appreciate your parents until you're alone and sick and there's no one to take care of you.*

I was not sick. But the world outside my apartment was.

It was days after the country declared a national lockdown, days after my university, an American university based in central Rome, had announced the beginning of an emergency "spring break" after the study abroad students were sent home.

Before the world went into pandemic-mode, I had done a crappy job of staying in touch with my parents. We went months without talking on the phone, and relied on Facebook Messenger for most of our communication. Though I felt slightly guilty about leaving them with an "empty nest" (my older sister, now 30, was long gone from my parent's house), I kept telling myself that we would see each other in summer. *Summer* would bring us closer. In *summer* I would finally be a good daughter again. In *summer* I would let my parents know how much I appreciated them.

When the lockdown started, I was overcome by a sense of despair. The future was uncertain, and I didn't know when I would be with my family again. There were so many things I had wanted to do that seemed so distant now: bake cookies with my mom, play Scrabble with my dad, go on kayaking trips down the river together. Those things were meant to bond us back together, to rebuild the bridges that the ocean between us had damaged.

Simultaneously, I was afraid for them. Even though they were tucked away in the mountains of rural Virginia, I worried for their health and safety. I felt a certain responsibility to be there to take care of them. My worst fear in the world was that *they* would be alone and sick, with no one to take care of *them*.

That first day of the lockdown, I called them. We video-chatted over breakfast (my breakfast, their happy hour). Over pre-packaged cornetti and sugar-less coffee, I urged them to stay home and not worry about me. They nodded back at me through the phone screen, their faces blurred by distance and bad WiFi.

The conversations started out slow, here and there, revolving around the coronavirus, the safety precautions I was taking, and whether or not I should try to fly home. My sister joined the calls too. Newly pregnant, she worried I would get 'stuck' in Italy and miss the baby's birth. Still uncertain about the future and whether my university would be able to reopen, I chose to stay.

Overtime, our conversations became livelier, about gossip from my hometown, meals we were cooking, or TV shows we were all watching. Calling them became part of my daily lockdown routine. For the first time since leaving my home the previous summer, I felt like I was part of my family again.

After nearly a month of lockdown, I decided to fly home. The decision was seamless. Being with my family was the right thing to do. I couldn't believe I had ever thought it wasn't.

On the plane ride home, with my mandatory mask tightly pulled over my face and my hands trapped in their latex gloves, it drifted back into my mind: *You will never appreciate your parents until you're alone and sick and there's no one to take care of you.*

No. For me it wasn't true. For me, it was the threat that we would all be alone and sick, unable to take care of each other, that brought me back home. What a waste that would be, I realized.

Margaret Kovick is a university student and freelance writer currently obtaining her bachelor's degree in English and Journalism. Her passions include international travel, food, pop culture, and social justice.

RICHARD A. MORAN

A Letter to Ann Patchett During COVID

Dear Ann,

About COVID. It is important that we know each other because if my wife dies before me, you are the only one in the world she has given me permission to marry, should I choose to ever remarry. Her opinion is based on her meeting you once during one of your book tours through San Francisco. I couldn't make your talk that night but she came home from the lecture and declared, "When I die, I found someone you can marry. Ann Patchett!" She has not repeated that sentence since that night.

I should note before we get too far along that, in spite of the anxiety of coronavirus, my wife and I are both currently in good health and we love each other. If all the virus predictions and actuarial tables are correct, I am sure I will die before her – but, nonetheless, I want to get on your radar. We are both big fans of you and your writing, but my interest in your work has particularly expanded since I now have that permission slip.

The allowance to be with you comes from my wife's love and concern for me. She neither has a death wish nor any interest in breaking up your marriage. She fears that if she goes first, I will be buried under casseroles from all the women around here who she believes might be after me. I doubt that will be the case, but I give her credit for some forward thinking. The other alternative is that I will be heartbroken and lonely. It seems only you can save me.

When I've mentioned to people that I might marry you the first reaction is, "Well, at least she is age appropriate." No comment on your writing skills, or questions about how it will all work, or how we met. The most important factor is that I am not about to marry someone in her twenties. Your photo on the back fold of the book jacket of *The Dutch House* tells me that we could be a match that others will approve; at least age-wise.

You never can tell how these things go. I know both men and women who say, "I'll never find love again like I had with (the dead person)". Next thing I know they are married and, to everyone's surprise, seem really happy. Then again, others who always seemed really unhappy in their marriage never remarry and seem even unhappier.

Most couples never have 'the talk' about romance after death. It's hard to imagine a spouse being with someone else in the biblical sense. I have threatened haunting any newly formed relationships but the details of how that would work for me are unclear. Discussions about death are difficult enough without bringing up sex and marriage. Maybe couples expect they will die on the same day. I suspect that rarely happens unless it's a murder/suicide, which is not on the list of anyone I know.

As we age, we prepare for financial options and every possible health possibility – but nothing about love after death. And to make things worse, men are not great planners. Guys tend to wake up each day and say, "What's for breakfast?" and will never consider, "What should I do after she is no longer with me?" The path forward is too ambiguous and uncharted. We leave a will, but no instructions about relationships. It's hard to imagine an addendum to the trust with an approved list of potential spouses. It's easier to imagine a list of those who are never to be seen again. Maybe we need post-nuptial agreements.

The paradox of being older is that we don't want to be lonely, but neither do we want to be heartbroken again. It's a risk either way, isn't it? Sometimes, we have to choose between bad options. To compound the paradox, any activity with a high degree of difficulty is off the list. Dating is one of those activities.

In a recent discussion with a ninety-year-old, I said, "I will visit you, I don't want you to be lonely." Her response was, "Everyone my age is lonely." We live in fear of being lonely but don't do very much about it because it's just too emotional and difficult. After being with someone you love for a long time it's hard to imagine being with someone else, but we can use our imaginations and come up with a plan.

I wish I had your knack for telling stories and developing characters who are so alive. I wonder if you ever fall in love with your characters and wish they could come alive like Pinocchio. Maybe this note will make it into one of your stories. I feel like I know you through your writing. And if you read any of my books you might understand what it takes to make a productive workplace. My writing is all non-fiction and hits a nerve about jerk bosses and such.

I hope my wife outlives me by many years, but consider yourself warned.

Please take care of yourself and practice social distancing until we might meet.

Your friend, and admirer,

Richard Moran is a San Francisco based writer, investor and wine maker. He is best known as an evangelist for common sense in business and can be heard weekly on CBS radio.

QUARANTINE & ISOLATION:

ROOPAL BADHEKA

IN SEARCH OF BOREDOM, FOR SALVATION

It could be Friday or Monday. I haven't the feel of the days or weeks anymore. Each day lingers, one after the next. I wake up, drink coffee, work on my writing or the garden, and end the day with a book in hand or eyes on a screen. Time accepts its irrelevance by hiding in the shadows.

It is hot in Houston, and yet there are these wonderful cool breezes, an unexpected quarantine benefit. As every automobile stopped, a gentle breeze unfurled. Mother Nature toys with our sanity by fighting us and rewarding all at once. But otherwise, it doesn't much feel like summer. When social distancing is the primary objective, a full-fledged summer barbeque does not have a chance. Some friends will venture, smiles hidden behind a mask. Others wave from afar, their boldness not willing or already shattered by fate. My family in NJ might as well be in France. Quarantines limit interstate road trips and despite the deals that United tempts, flying is too dangerous.

Effectively, there are no get-togethers. The opposite is happening. We are getting even more disconnected. We are both ensconced and craving our own space like never before. Two months into some form of quarantine, we are tired of Zoom, FaceTime, and Webex. We are tired of Netflix, Hulu, and the internet. We are tired of being home. Now stuck in the monotony of our everyday lives, what is left to drive our lives?

Will we finally get to the place that meditation begged us to get to? Sitting alone, quietly in a room, every thought dropping effortlessly to the floor? Will we finally be able to sit in silence?

It's a fair bet that Mother Nature has a plan. And we can go kicking and screaming but the path is a fait accompli. Thousands of lost lives validate that story each day. But what of us that remain, do we know the grand plan? Perhaps, the same way we teach our kids the alphabet (sometimes kicking and screaming) so that they can learn to read Fitzgerald and write like Hemingway, Mother Nature guides our tutelage too.

The more time we spend solo, the more we learn to listen to ourselves. The more we adjust to the space of bare social calendars and eventless evenings, the more time we have to think clearly. The more we hear about a virus that impacts our lungs, the more we listen to ourselves breathe. The more we quarantine, the more we crave walking outside.

Any stress relief journal will recite those same recommendations for stress relief: *walking in nature, the space to think, breathing deeply, and meditating.* Ironic?

We started this journey filled with stress. As this virus continues to perpetuate, we will continue in our cocoons. We will adjust, maybe twist and turn. We will shed social conditioning and norms. We will abandon ties and work schedules. But what emerges at the end of this cycle? What radical transformation will take place? Who will we become?

Maybe we were known only as parents and will emerge as teachers and playmates for our children. Maybe we were once only consumers and will emerge as farmers of our land. Maybe we entered as employees and will emerge as entrepreneurs in the new economy. When confronted with silence, we must ask ourselves. What do we want to be at the end of this? What essence, tone, and color are the butterflies we will become?

Everything without change is tedious. It is so with relationships, jobs, the school year, books, hobbies, and places. Add the word new to any of them and excitement is born. During this time, it isn't enough to start a new hobby, cook new food, or learn a new language. Doing laundry by fabric vs. color is not enough.

The real question before us is, what new thinking can we do?

The blank slate of life stands before us. A piece of fresh white chalk in our hands is restless and free to write. What does the future entail? What new hope or dream will we have solved, figured out, made whole?

2020 is a time of perfect vision.

Clarity is ours. Everything about this time restricts our body, not our minds. What is the new thing our mind is asking for? Peace, tranquility, or adventure and excitement? A chance to rest or a chance to vie for freedom, equality, and success? A bounty of fortune or a bounty of new friends? Finding a partner or searching for independence? Losing our faith or challenging our beliefs?

The choice is ours and finally, since we're not texting, commuting, watching, calling, attending, or flying, we have plenty of time to figure it out. Since we are resting, being, existing, sheltering, separating, and isolating, we have plenty of space to figure it out. In other words, boredom will prove to be the savior that awakens humanity to a brand-new era, and the butterfly that emerges is the one that has been awakened.

A Jersey girl, who's a Texan at heart, after living in Houston for two decades, Roopal Badheka is a screenwriter and writer. Her drama and romantic comedy feature screenplays have garnered multiple film festival awards and finalist placements. Her literary fiction has also been featured in such publications as The Wanderlust Journal, A Long Story Short, *and others. She writes a bi-monthly motivational blog for her writing, consulting, and coaching company.*

JERIANN HILDERLEY

TO BE EXTRA-ORDINARY

April 3. (BC is Before COVID-19 and DC, During COVID-19). Can I distinguish my 82-year-old self (BC) from the anxious, discombobulated person I have become (DC)? I have the same need to feed, heal, and inspire others with my work. But I have been bent out of shape by the new procedures my partner Janet and I have to follow. Operating primarily in digital space with everyone else is disorienting.

So much of our time is taken up with obtaining food. BC I shopped and easily found what I needed at several markets. Now we're limited to where and what items can be ordered. Obtaining cleaning and medical supplies has similar angst. "Shit! They don't have Clorox Wipes!" My brand of 'dry eye' drops never seemed so precious. We're using ever-smaller pieces of paper towel for napkins. Yet home-cooked meals with Janet give comfort and mirror our life BC.

How do we stay healthy, keep the lurking virus out of our tiny studio? Because of our age and health, we don't go *outside*, a word with new meaning. *Outside* now is hallway, elevator, stairs to lobby, lobby itself (where we retrieve deliveries and mail) and laundry room. Every time we step beyond our doorway, we don *outside* shoes and clothes, masks and Nitrile gloves. Each trip to the garbage disposal at the end of the hall requires Corona gear. Availability of supplies determines how and when we use them. I remember the rationing of butter, sugar, and eggs during WWII in my small midwestern hometown. Now it's toilet paper, paper towels, cleanser and hand sanitizer.

We are relieved when we can order basic food supplies, but we NEED cookies! What if our market has no more milk and (yikes!) oatmeal raisin cookies? Janet nicknamed me "Scarcity" (spelled Scare-City).

Our BC *outside* is no longer. I think of prisoners confined for years, especially those in solitary. Our situation can't be compared; when freedom is suddenly jeopardized, even slightly, we find new compassion for those suffering from homelessness, famine, repression, and imprisonment. We need a recess from this cloistered space. Just fifteen minutes of fresh air and nature's company. Fragments from the past, angst in the present, and fears of the future suffocate me. Maybe if we walk strategically, warily with our masks, we can make it to Riverside Park. I can't lighten up; I am pressed down.

How can I handle COVID-19 despair at 82? These microscopic parasites are killing thousands daily, mainly poor people of color. (A few white celebrities too.) I'm learning how capitalism encourages the trajectory of this slaughter. Every day we are finding out more of the virus' destructive capabilities, not only to lungs, but also to heart and brain. It works in devious, unclear ways. Are those who have survived it immune to future *attacks*? (Didn't we say *bouts* of the flu?) Can they still carry the virus? How can I dispel morbid thoughts and fatigue? How long will this last? Are we taking enough precautions? Janet says we must order a pulse oximeter to measure oxygen saturation of our blood.

Could this pandemic world be our new norm? How do we preserve our creative spirits? Will I still be able to make a difference? Will we keep getting food, medicines, cleaning supplies? More immediately: will we find a way to really go *outside* and be safe? Can the new hard lessons teach us how to become more humane? Conquering the pandemic requires social distancing, owning our responsibility to respect and protect every human being, including us. The charts of the areas and populations hit the hardest are proof of deliberate, on-going, government-backed racism in the U.S.

May 3. How else has this pandemic warfare changed me? I have worked life-long to be nurturing, politically active, creative and productive, (without patriarchal blessings); I strive to keep growing. After reassuring myself BC that the unpublished novels, short stories and essays I've written in the last decades can be of value to others, I was diligently researching and submitting work to publishing venues. Then, wham! Along comes this life-changing, dream-changing, ambition changing.... I can't find the words to name this serial killer Behemoth! I am blind-sided.

This virus-crisis has made me even more upset about my age. Can I still write something of value for others? I hope this journal will help me figure out how to be of service. A crisis of this magnitude requires enormous struggle to comprehend! And then I interject my own insecurities? What an indulgence! I'll try harder.

May 14. Remember: Engaged, focused work and activities, writing, reading, cooking, Zoom webinars, a streamed concert, FaceTiming with a friend distract me from fretting. I can still learn! Even the damn scourge recedes momentarily.

May 18. Remember: People of all ages are dying not only from this virus, but from poverty, discrimination, our government's sanctions. Be thankful that Janet and I are alive, in decent health. During this profoundly hard period for so many, meditate on how best to use the precious time I still have on this planet. Be thankful for my interests, skills, energy, pension check, medical coverage, a home, loved ones, family, partner, comrades. Let my writing call out for a safer, more empathic and just world for everyone. Work with others to build a healthy earth-home for all inhabitants.

Mindful work, alone and with others, helps transform destructive, obsessive ruminations into constructive actions. I just told Janet my name is "sagacity!" Remember: I can work to be extra-ordinary *because* of my age.

Though I have worked in several media – sculpture, street theater, music, and now the writing of memoir-driven novels – all my creative works have evolved out of the vital social/political/cultural issues of their times. Thus, I call myself an artist-activist concerned with seeking unique ways to address injustice, inequality, disabling viruses, as I work with others for the good of all and the caretaking of our earth-home.

LAURA PREBLE

EMPTY NEST

Mrs. Finch is gone again.

She hasn't been home since yesterday afternoon when my dogs barked and scared her into flying off the patio and into a guava tree. She's a bird, so I'm sure she knows how to take care of herself, but still, I worry.

She and her husband (finches mate for life) decided to build a nest in one of our patio ceiling fans, a burnished brass industrial thing with an Edison bulb in it. The pair first started to build the nest in the fan closest to the patio door, but abandoned it since we came in and out so often. They moved over to the next fan on the patio ceiling, but she still bolts when she hears the door lock turn.

My excessive finch monitoring is a byproduct of my inaction. Since the pandemic, I've been home all the time. I had submitted my retirement paperwork in early January, before Wuhan became a household word. I'd planned on leaving my high school librarian job at the end of June. But I left in March, and never came back. One day I was working, greeting all the students who drifted into my book haven, talking to teachers who came to use the copier, trying to get help shelving books. And then suddenly, I was no longer there. School shut down. No one knew what to do.

It's been almost five months now. I have diabetes and auto-immune conditions, and I'm almost 60, so I don't take chances with this virus. I live in a science-denying community where masks are a political statement, so I don't go out. I've been to the pharmacy four times, picked up takeout food twice, and driven my car so the battery doesn't die. I'm still on the same tank of gas I had when we started lockdown. I'm not complaining; I love home. But there is this disconnection, this great wide gulf between me and everyone else except my immediate family. Zoom meetings and phone calls don't really satisfy.

I suppose that's why I started to notice the birds. I have a lovely, large yard, so I walk it in the morning before the Southern California sun scorches the pavement in the afternoon. The finches, though, are right there, visible from my sofa. Every morning, I wake up, get some coffee, and check on their status.

This morning, I don't see her, the mama. I call her Mrs. Finch. She had several eggs in the nest, and her husband, Mr. Finch, visited once or twice a day. I know when he's there because they have a very lively conversation, maybe about the quality of our worms, or about the lack of accessible drinking water. She does most of the talking.

I did a little research, so I know the chicks should hatch after about 14 days. I've been watching and waiting, increasingly distressed when I see mama gone. It's warm out, so I guess she doesn't have to sit on the eggs all the time, but as a mother, I question her dedication.

If I leave the patio door open just a bit, my dogs can still get out but Mrs. Finch doesn't fly away in a panic. The dogs and even my cat don't seem to bother her with their comings and goings; it's only the door, the lock, the human element that terrifies her.

I sit, watching the slips of weeds hanging from the nest as they move listlessly. No sound comes from there. No baby birds.

I worry about where she is. I worry about whether some gang of feral cats or a red-tailed hawk might have spirited her away. Is the father waiting too? Is he watching from a tree, nervous? Do birds get nervous?

There are so many things I notice now that I didn't notice then. We have a pool, and my husband and I have taken to rescuing honeybees that accidentally dive in. We take an old snorkel and fish them out, gently place them on the concrete, and watch eagerly to see if they will fly away, or if they're dead.

We look at our roses every day, noting which are starting to sprout new blooms. We grow spinach, but we are lousy suburban farmers, so it has all gone to seed. I notice orb weaver spiders that have strung death traps for tinier bugs off our lampposts. I've named the two spiders. One is Roy Orbison and one is Orbille Wright.

Butterflies move in pairs, dancing through the air. I never knew that butterflies mated, although I guess it explains why we still have butterflies. I'd just never seen it in action, the graceful dance that they do above the purple butterfly bushes. And baby lizards! I knew, I guess, that lizards had babies, but I'd never seen any miniature ones until now.

Mrs. Finch still isn't back, and I'm on my second cup of coffee. What can I do? A search party? I can't climb the eucalyptus trees. She blends in, like the cotton-tailed rabbits do when they stand, frozen, on the grass if I walk outside. They're all so afraid of humans.

We're not so different. I'm afraid of humans too.

I really hope Mrs. Finch comes back. I'm going to cry for the baby birds and Mr. Finch if she doesn't.

Laura Preble is an author and educator. Her most recent novel, Anna Incognito, *has won several awards. She is also the author of the* Queen Geek Social Club *series.*

AMY GELFMAN

CROWNING A NEW DAY

Remember the day the world came to a halt?
And we all pointed fingers shouting "who is at
fault?"
We may never know, though hard we may try,
the who or the when or the how or the why.

They said stay at home, be safe, don't go out!
Most people abided, others started to shout.
Their sense of certainty and control, lost in confusion; but,
   in fact it was never there - it's all an illusion.

Still, some counted their blessings, enjoying their life,
alone in their home with their kids and their wife.
With patience and caring, they all lived with less.
As long as the family was happy, "let's not mind the
   mess."

No shopping, or movies, or a nice restaurant date.
A new situation tested our fate.
Kids put down their devices and got on their bikes.
Mom and dad packed up lunches and took nature hikes.
No meetings to run to, few errands to do,
Brought more joy than expected to more than a few.

But others were lonely at home in their bed.
Anxiety growing 'bout what lie ahead.
The unknown, a dark cloud, of worrisome matter,
Of ruinous outcomes and meaningless chatter.

Our loved ones alone? Unimaginable at best.
When suffering ended, many were laid to rest...
Without a gathering to celebrate their life and hear all their
    stories,
Of their triumphs and strife and momentous glories.

My friends, the story, has and will take its toll.
And teach us the things for which we've no control.
We can't stop the wind as it fiercely blows by
or the break of the waves or a baby's soft cry.

But all is not helpless and this too shall pass.
We won't always wave to each other through glass.
Soon we will dance on the street, from our homes we will
    race!
Embracing each other, at last face-to-face.

If one tiny, invisible virus makes havoc worldwide,
think of the impact we can make if only we tried.
So if the wind is too strong, we can shelter each other.
We can finally reach out to our father and mother.

If the waves overwhelm in the ocean so vast,
we can choose a safe haven and break free at last.
If you happen to hear a baby's soft cries,
Open your arms and you'll soon realize...

That you matter! You count in this world where we live...

where we've taken so much, now it's time that we give!
With good health and compassion we'll pave a new way...
For our children and grandchildren on this very day.
Instead of corona, we'll crown one another.
Imagine the blessings of joy we'll discover!

I am a wife and mother (six boys) first and foremost. In between the cracks and crevices of home life, I create folk and Judaica art and sing with seniors with dementia and Alzheimer's. Music, humor and art are my way of channeling love and creating connections with my fellow human beings.

Painting by Amy Gelfman

DARLA SMITH

2020 – THE UNINTENTIONAL YEAR OF RAINBOWS AND SUCK

When considering 2020 thus far, it would be easy to focus only on the negative: the COVID-19 panic, the subsequent crumbling economy, the shoddy, agenda-driven media hype, the dangerous levels of vitriol being hurled about by dueling political parties, eternal finger pointing, Twitter fights, the looming Presidential election, the constant threat of violence being perpetrated upon hard-working taxpayers by blue-haired, participant-trophy-recipient rioters that appear to have soy IVs in their arms, the heartbreaking murder of George Floyd, the frothing-at-the-mouth mob mentality, the establishment of CHAZ/CHOP in Seattle, the impending doom of death by murder hornets, asphyxiation thanks to Sahara dust storms, and, obviously, the final countdown to either the zombie apocalypse or alien invasion.

But I have decided to be positive. This is possibly because I have lost my mind in 2020. I think it is more so because I don't know what else to do – it's either look for the proverbial silver lining in this shit show or rip my hair out, and I have great hair, so screw that. I'm digging for unicorn nuggets, friends.

Yes, China sucks ginormous donkey testicles for *creating* and spreading this hideous virus. (Adjusts tinfoil hat.) But how did its rampant release and spread truly affect my family?

Well, on St. Patty's day, a day that should have been filled with consuming copious amounts of green beer and corned beef hash, I was fired from my job. First time in my life I have ever lost a job. I was dumbfounded and numb after that extremely uncomfortable phone call.

I had to file for unemployment. The PA unemployment site was sorely unequipped to handle the gushing levels of new claims. Five weeks later I was finally able to obtain my unemployment compensation, but many other folks were still waiting and terrified.

It was scary. I was hurt, bewildered, angry, shocked, frustrated.

But you know what? (Rainbow alert, people...) I ended up being fine.

I took more walks with my dog. I spent time with my sons. I taught my younger boy how to bake chocolate chip cookies. I worked with both boys on laundry perfection. I cleaned my house. I slept in. I caught up on some binge-watching of shows I was interested in but just hadn't had time to explore yet.

My husband moved his office into our formal dining room. We started spending time together in the evenings, taking long walks with the dog. We ate lunch together every day for the first time in our 23-year marriage. We talked more. I cooked wholesome, healthy meals.

I ate a lot and gained ten lbs. (Trust me, that is not a unicorn nugget. Just a side effect of happiness and good food.)

We giggled as one of our cats, Baby, positioned herself firmly on top of whichever pile of papers my husband needed most for work. Baby has a perpetually runny nose caused by a constant upper respiratory infection. The vet has given up attempting to cure it after all these years. *It just is.*

She loves to leave giant snot globules in the most inconvenient spots for her Hoomans to find at the most inconvenient of times. My husband's work Zoom-mates got a kick out of watching Baby saunter past the computer camera, plop herself down with her asshole in my husband's nose, and spew a fountain of slimy nose grease all over his makeshift office.

It's gross, but it's funny. And God knows, we need some funny in 2020.

I've interviewed more in the last four months than I have in my entire life. Interviews are interesting. They seem to flow along a very harsh pendulum swing. They were one of two types of discussions: Type One – Let's talk about your resume and background and then I'll tell you a bit about the job and you can ask me questions. Type Two – Take a personality test, jump through these hoops, stand on your head and recite the Declaration of Independence, and then answer ninety questions about your favorite color and the worst thing you've ever eaten.

But guess what? Rainbows! I got two job offers and accepted and finalized one this week.

Of course, I tripped and broke my right shoulder 15 days ago.

I wish I could say I was going 95 on a motorcycle or that I had enough of these Antifa antics and I sucker punched a pimply-faced nerd right in his miniscule ballsack and that's how I hurt myself, but no.

I was picking herbs.

It was my older son's 20th birthday. I had 25,000 steps already recorded on my FitBit, and was sweaty and dirty after having push-mowed our lawn, my car was packed to the brim with Goodwill donations, I needed to run to the grocery store, and I had to grab some fresh lemon thyme from my driveway earthboxes for my salmon marinade.

This is what happens when busy 50-year-old women get clumsy.

My feet tangled up with a driveway downspout and I slammed into the concrete with the full force of my newly enhanced weight, squarely on my right shoulder. I knew immediately it was broken because it HURT LIKE A MOTHERFUCKER.

But guess what? Silver lined rainbow with dancing unicorns dropping golden nuggets from their glittering buttholes, people.

The break was straight and clean. No need for surgery.

I've been in a sling, sleeping upright for 15 days. I'm healing beautifully. I write like a two-year-old on acid with my left hand. Seriously, I couldn't make this shit up if I tried. The broken shoulder sucks. This year sucks. Coronavirus sucks. Gaining happy weight sucks.

It all SUCKS. And yet, I'm fine. My family is fine. My animals are freaking great – they love having 24/7 access to their Hoomans. The world is slowly opening back up. The economy is creeping heavenward again.

Drink some good wine. Talk with some great friends. Laugh at something. Get some rest. You'll be fine, too.

Darla has been lucky in her half century of living. She shares life with two amazing sons, a sweet husband, an insane dog, and three adorable cats. She has made a living out of selling great products that make people's lives better. In her spare time she likes to claim she eats Keto (while munching on tortilla chips), loves spending time with close friends and a chilled glass of Prosecco, and believes that a good, hearty laugh is better than any anti-depressant a doctor could prescribe.

Robin Seideman

Coronavirus Diaries

"Stop the world, I want to get off," has been my mantra for many years. And yet, when the world stopped, I continued with the momentum of a ball released from the end of a spinning string.

John Kabat-Zinn titled his book, *Wherever you go, There you are*. That's the burn. That's the blessing.

The 'me' with the skill set that struggles with organization and focus persisted; however, the 'me' who deeply appreciated every minute of bonus quality time with those I love deepened.

I didn't meditate every day.
I didn't write all those cards and notes I planned to.
I didn't file all my receipts.
I didn't paint any pictures.
I didn't journal.
I didn't lose the weight.
I didn't clean out my closet.

I sat on my swing each day.
I communed with the growing family of bunnies in my yard.
I grew tomatoes, basil and marigolds.
I walked.

I cooked nutritious meals.
I Zoom cocktail-partied each Saturday night with my
    family.
I went to the beach.
I supported my neighbors.
I sewed masks.
I taught my son basic carpentry.
I organized my garage.
I got enough sleep.
I put flower magnets on my car.

The mundane has become even more precious.

I appreciate my health and the health of those I love even
    more.
I am even more grateful for my dear family, friends and
    community.
I am grateful for how small our planet has become.
I am grateful for the privilege to comfort those who grieve.
I am grateful for my teachers, mentors and guides.
I am grateful to all those in professions who save lives,
    feed others, keep our environment clean and safe.
I am grateful for forgiveness and reunions.
I am simply more deeply grateful.

May G-d bless the souls of those who we lost, bless the
    mourners, bless those on the front lines.
May we merit a speedy end to this plague.

Robin is an educator, artist and healer.

Dr. Alessandra Rosa

Social Distancing

This art piece represents the uncertainty and stress experienced during the quarantine due to COVID-19. I live in the United States with my husband and son, but our family members are in Spain and Puerto Rico. Our worrying intensified when seeing news of cases increasing in all of the three locations. Similarly, acknowledging the saddening fact that we might not see each other physically for almost a whole year!

Dr. Alessandra Rosa is a Postdoctoral scholar in the Department of Sociology at University of South Florida. As a Puerto Rican she has dedicated her teaching, research, and service to fostering diversity, equity, and justice. Her research centers on social movements, Internet activism, education, Puerto Rican studies, post-disaster migration studies, emotional well-being, and discourse analysis.

Painting by Dr. Alessandra Rosa

DANIELA MATZ

TURNING 13 IN QUARANTINE

My experience in the COVID-19 pandemic has been extremely memorable, and something that I will always remember and pass on when I am older. I remember the day at school when our teachers asked us to pack our things and say goodbye to all our friends since school was being shut down. We all cheered with excitement since we were missing class, but little did I know that I would actually miss school in the future.

The first days of coronavirus were pretty interesting and confusing. First off, I couldn't really see any of my friends, and I hated having to call them all the time to socialize. Second, all my classes were on this app I had never heard of called Zoom, and from then on, I would have to use it for the rest of the year. I truly thought that the pandemic would last for a week and we would all be back in school after then, so me and my friends would watch YouTube after our classes, go to school in our pajamas, and even joke about the coronavirus like it was no big deal.

Eventually I realized that I would be in school for way longer than I thought, and online school was definitely getting old. It was also extremely hard to stay in touch with my friends, and I would often feel lonely since I had forgotten to call them or just didn't feel like it. Our teachers were all extremely kind to us during school, none of our tests counted, and we didn't have any finals or ERBs. It was nice to be able to slack off a little bit, but it was also super hard to stay entertained and have fun at home.

After school was finally over, it was summer and I started to see my friends more. At first they came to my house and we would social distance in the backyard, but we would start to go places like the mall and the beach, so my parents would restrict things more. It was so frustrating when my friends would invite me to go to the park or to hang out at Century City Mall and I had to say no, but it would help my family stay away from the virus and help them stay safe.

Life is just so difficult when you have to watch every move you make to make sure you don't get sick, and it's super annoying when you can't see your best friends because your parents are extra overprotective about the virus. I even had to have my birthday in quarantine, which was fun but not the same as going to Disneyland or something like that.

Something that people don't understand is that it's already so difficult being a teenager, so being a teenager in quarantine with parents who are extra concerned about the pandemic is no picnic. I'm not going to lie to you and say that my experience has been fun, because it has been the exact opposite. But it has taught me to value more important things than my friends in life, and to treasure this historic experience that I have been through.

Daniela Matz is a 13-year-old from Los Angeles who loves baking, reading, writing and fashion.

STACY OXLEY

LOOKING FORWARD

A breath-taking sunrise
Of ripening love, warming
Embittered hearts amid
Metallic beats, cast in
Consuming shadows.

Contrasting colours of
Twin reflections staring,
Birthing a blossoming
Yearning of tenderly
Reaching fingertips.

Placing smooth palms
Upon cooling glass,
Accompanying a
Sparrow songstress,
Barely heard.

Heedless hearts of
Loving souls apart
But longing to
Entwine, smiling in
Unspoken joy of future
Promises.

Lit by a soulful glow
Of an aspiring spring,
Awakening from bare
Walls of winter wilds,

Housed under aging
Slate of nurturing
Guardians.

I love the season of Autumn, and I more than admire the beauty of the written word - devastating, brash, inspiring, courageous and always artful. Horses are one of my ruling passions their strength, beautiful spirit and grace are more than I dare to describe. Mother nature is my greatest inspiration for writing, and at times my one true solace.

ESTRELLA A. DATO

FROM COVID-19 DIARY

MARCH 15, 2020

Community lockdown begins today. No land, air, or sea
travels to and from the capital city of Manila, from March 15
to April 14.

I am locked out, holed up here in Graceland Tayabas,
a gated resort, a lavish 11-hectare development inside a
22-hectare property development. Paranoia is setting in
but I am trying to make sense of this pandemic: maybe a
correction, a warning? I am confident this shall soon pass.
Besides, I only have a month to go. I am scheduled to fly out,
back to Canada on April 16.

MARCH 18, 2020

Today is the fourth day of my self-quarantine. I have
started my regimen of walking. Safe distancing is a piece
of cake. The resort is closed; no check-ins. I only saw one
solitary jogger and two guys fishing in the lagoon. The
resort's restaurant is closed, too.

MARCH 20, 2020

After five days of self-isolation, I need to go out. My
prepaid internet connection is expiring; I need to buy some
supplies. I was stopped at the gate. Why is there a barricade?

I was told no one can go out or in without a quarantine pass. *A what?*

A quarantine pass is issued by the *barangay* — a political unit of local government in the Philippines — a prerequisite for the mandated community lockdown. I don't even know where to get the pass, or how. But I need to go to the town centre, my internet connection is expiring. I don't care about food, but no internet? It has been my only connection to the outside world. Omeegee, physically isolated and internet disconnected, double whammy! My protestations were unheeded. No quarantine pass, no in or out.

I used the remaining few hours of internet connection to warn my friends and family that I shall soon be out of commission. It was like a cry for help!

Yikes, an email received: April 16 flight has been cancelled! Another one: European tour in September to see the Passion Play in Oberammergau, Germany, also cancelled.

The world is closing in on me. Ugggh.

My phone was pinging all evening. Text messages, last-ditch efforts by friends, offering support. The first responder is my friend Mila. My neighbour on the fourth floor offered to help me with the pass.

Just like that, my troubles seem to be dissipating. This day is not a total loss.

MARCH 22, 2020

I am feeling hopeful today. It is springtime in the prairies. I envision my perennial garden in Saskatoon coming to life, though snow is probably not gone yet. I remember why I love escaping harsh Canadian prairie winter here: the sun is shining, the sky is blue. Warming up, but there is a soft breeze coming from the Sierra mountain ranges.

I got my internet connected, hurray. An email confirmed that our cancelled flight is rescheduled. I got my pass with the help of my neighbor. Like giddy 'escaped' prisoners, we were permitted to go out even if it is not our 'official' day-out. She gave me a ride to the town centre; we bought our *pandesal* and some supplies. Like ships passing in the night, we've been meeting at the elevator and the hallways before with a hi and a simple smile of recognition. Today, we exchanged mobile phone numbers. I just made a friend.

MARCH 28, 2020

With my pass, I thought I could go to Lucena, the city capital, about 12 kilometres away, and visit my brother and family. With my pass, and with mask on, I went through three checkpoints manned by police and the military. I was refused passage at the last checkpoint, where I can see the gate of my brother's house. I tried to reason. I pleaded. I offered to park my car and just walk to pick up a medication and be back right away. The civilian volunteer hailed a superior, a uniformed soldier. But he turned his back and rudely walked away without saying a word. The civilian volunteer apologized for him, '*Pasensya po*'. Rejected, dejected, fuming, I seriously felt like crashing through that barricade. But instead, I made a U-turn and drove away. *Pasensya,* reverberating in my head.

Trying to calm myself down, I appease myself with that same word instead. *Pasensya* — a word that I hear a lot here in the Philippines, a word that irked me. I have always thought of it as an excuse for incompetence. *Pasensya* is a Filipino universal excuse for everything. Not just a plain sorry, it is humbly asking for patience and understanding, endurance, perseverance. I am less of a Canadian today; I am more a humbled Filipino.

MAY 24, 2020

Today is Ascension Day. There will be mass streaming on Facebook and on TV later. I have been missing the solemnity of the actual mass and the solace the church offers. While on my early morning walk, I heard church bells ringing, as if calling out to me. Not my day pass today, but the heck with it! I went out to investigate. The small chapel down Graceland road is closed. I drove down to the centuries-old Tayabas Basilica Minore. The gates are closed, too.

JUNE 23, 2020

Marking my 100th day of observing self-isolation and solitary walks today. There have been annoyances and inconveniences but I am grateful I am safe and healthy here.

I find so many positive elements. The world seems greener. The birds are flying lower. The people I met are friendlier, more understanding. Less cars, less traffic. Quiet. COVID-19 is not all evil, there are lessons to be learned.

I am packing up a storm, hoping that our flight on July 1 is a go. Scheduled to arrive in Vancouver on Canada Day. I wonder what is waiting for me on the other side of the Pacific.

After 100 days of self-quarantine here in Tayabas Graceland, I am mandated to go on a 14-day quarantine once I arrive in Saskatoon. Bring it on.

I am retired, and divide my time between Canada and the Philippines.

Courtney Yount

Smiling Through Quarantine

When I toasted to the new year saying, "I have 20/20 vision", this was not the vision I imagined. It was quite the opposite, honestly. What I imagined to be the most amazing start to the next decade of the twenty-first century ended up turning into a never-ending dark tunnel. However, after my anxiety subsided, and I looked up at the stars after the first week of quarantine praying for God to release my fears and worries about the future, I realized it's not so dark after all.

I have always been a person of optimism and a bright-side seeker in every situation, and my faith has always been a leading force for that upward mindset. During the time the world shut down, I was blessed to be confined in the same four walls as my parents in the always beautiful state of Maine. While at first it was a bit of an adjustment to not be able to get out much, and our jobs were either put on pause or moved online, we were able to get time together that we never really had, or paid attention to, when we were living on fast forward, constantly racing in and out the door, but always remembering to say "I love you" after each "Goodbye". We had movie days and tried new recipes in the kitchen; if they took all day and ended up getting burnt or destroyed, we still had smiles on our faces. We held onto each other tighter than ever because at the time, the thought of hugging someone 'from the outside' was like begging for an infection. I probably wouldn't have made it through quarantine as easily if I didn't have them next to me at all times to keep me sane and to keep my mindset permanently upward.

When it was safer to venture out of the house, I made it a point to go for a walk through my neighborhood, or drive to the beach and just watch the waves crash onto the soft sand. Listening to how the waves were still as majestic, strong and powerful as they were before the world shut down gave me hope that we'll all come out of this strong and powerful. When the breeze hit my ears that first time I walked outside, it was as if Mother Nature was whispering to me, "It's going to be okay." I was able to really absorb the world around me, and not ignore it by staring at a computer or my phone all day like I usually would. I gained a higher appreciation for the trees and the ocean and the Earth; how generous she was to let us all reside in every nook and cranny of her being. The fresh air even seemed to taste sweeter.

I also made it a point to carve out time for my significant other, whether that was through FaceTime twice a week or meeting up every two weeks just to hug each other and feel each other in our arms again. Even though we couldn't see each other as often as we'd wanted to, and our future concert plans were cancelled, our love wasn't. We didn't grow apart during those weeks, and we didn't have any ounce of negativity seep into our relationship. We built each other up and we never stopped saying "I love you" every day. We kept our hope and our faith high, and we found the happiness in virtual dates and online co-op gaming. I'd say our love got a lot stronger during that difficult time.

My eyes were opened a lot during this pandemic as well. While being secluded in my room those couple months, I started to become more aware of the unrest in our country; not just the pandemic, but the racial injustice that has always been under our noses. I understood everything better, and I took the time to really educate myself and see where I could do better as a friend, as an American, and as a human. I made it a point to reach out to others, whether they were old friends or co-workers, and share my positivity and good wishes. I raised my voice and I listened during that time.

I reconnected with old friends that I haven't seen in years, because if I died today, I'd regret not telling them how much

I care for them and how much I miss them. We're already making plans to see each other when this pandemic has died and we are free from restrictions to hug each other, be near each other, and enjoy each other's company.

My job was put on hold when the pandemic started; I was laid off for two weeks and had to file for unemployment. I work for a local record/book/movie store in Maine, and it's definitely the best job with the best managers and co-workers I have ever had. They're like my second family. We were able to figure things out for us to meet over Zoom and find creative ways to stay connected to our customers and with each other. We hosted Twitch streams for new games, such as Animal Crossing, we made creative YouTube videos discussing our favorite movie/TV show/music picks for the week, and we smiled and laughed through the whole process, all while building each other up and keeping our spirits high. We built a stronger community together, and we found a greater appreciation for our jobs and our second family.

While this entire situation seems scary and may feel like we're in the middle of the unknown, it's important to find the silver linings in every day. I wrote in one of my blog posts to "not be afraid of slowing down". We've spent so much time on fast forward that we forgot what it feels like to really slow down and absorb the world around us. Absorb those relationships and create those adventures indoors and outdoors; love harder.

Stay safe and be healthy.

Writing has always been a big passion of mine. Honestly, it's like another limb for me. It gave me the strengths to find my own voice while being an introvert, and it has also helped shape me into who I am today. I hope to inspire the world through writing someday. Hopefully, I'm already inspiring others today.

ALAINA PEREZ

AFTERNOONS IN ISOLATION

Soaking on the porch
with banana bread and toast.
Two journals and someone else's tan on the wood.
Cheers to beers and nothingness,
and who would have thought that solace could find me
after being lost in the everything.
In the all the time.
I can hear the birds,
woodpeckers, robins.
Wistful songs in the willows,
surprisingly saccharine, and still.

Alaina Perez is a student, teacher, and hoarder of words. She is pursuing her Master's degree in English at Oakland University in Auburn Hills, Michigan.

DOMINICK DOMINGO

THINGS SEEN IN ALLEYS

Parched, buckled asphalt scored with gritty fissures and whitewashed by time heaves moonward, abducted by her pull, splitting and falling away, at last surrendering to gravity.

To remain like chapped urban lips, pursed at a buttermilk sky and taunting the tread of tires.

Of all the things lurking in hidden alleys, today's glimpse ranks highest—fleshy and diaphanous, catching sun

He brakes, second-hand cherry-red Schwinn grinding to a halt.

The world has yielded nothing familiar, for months— nothing *lifegiving*—only the promise of more: More withholding, more destitution, the fleeting memory of freedom, a shapeless reckoning licking a moonless night, like flames.

The horizon hosts but looming threats—of micro-invaders and police states and orange-haired assholes breathing lies to sheep.

Brown muck has settled, clearing the once-oppressive silt of sky and promising eternity.

Metal behemoths jet few and far between, assaulting the air with sputtering coughs of the brown muck that once blanketed all, horizon-to-horizon.

It's all that redeems this silence.

Nights, absent yuppies and hipsters, coyotes have the run of streets.

No touch, no connectivity, for months—only masks and gloves and distance, suspicion and insurmountable divide.

And if the world without is inept as a prison, his own cells mutiny, render themselves as prone to invaders as a flame to the slightest breeze: a year without touch.

And now this:

Sinewy arms peeling damp cotton from a lean torso, slick with sweat. All efficiency, no excess stored like toilet paper or Handi-wipes.

Only what's *essential*.

Dominick Domingo is a veteran Disney Feature Animation artist (Lion King, Pocahontas, Hunchback of Notre Dame, Tarzan, Fantasia) *who transitioned into live-action filmmaking. His award-winning narrative nonfiction essays and short stories have been included in anthologies. His Young Adult Fantasy trilogy* The Nameless Prince *launched in 2012 through Twilight Times Books and has been capturing imaginations since. Dominick resides in the Franklin Hills neighborhood of Los Angeles, and can be seen pecking away on his laptop in coffee shops on any given day.*

Janet Skiff

Hearing the Birds

When I took the dogs out last night, all was quiet, except for the clear repeated "hooing" of an owl from a nearby tree. Restaurants, bars and movie theaters in our university town have been closed for a month. There have been no sports or live performances since before spring break. No place to go with a pandemic in progress.

A neighbor called from across the street last week, "The birds sound louder now, don't you think?" "Maybe so," I answered with little thought. It has been on my mind since.

I'm here, at home, writing, gardening, finding ways to connect with people and keep things going that don't normally take place on my property. A quiet life.

The swirling calls of birds collecting at our feeder woke me this morning. I think they seem louder now because they're not drowned out by us and our machines; we stay inside more. The rumbling of delivery trucks is the main human sound. The shrills and chatter of children are no longer heard outside the nearby elementary school.

I have not seen the small red lights of jets flashing high against the black background of night, moving among the sparkling white and yellow dots of planets and stars. Few commercial planes have flown since the coronavirus became real to us. In the past when I've seen them after dark, I've imagined the dimmed cabin and sleepy passengers lulled by the thrum of engines and have blessed their journey, because

104

often I have been one of them. The sky also hung airliner-free just after 9/11.

In February I flew to Costa Rica for my oldest son's wedding and was hoping to travel in early spring from my home in Iowa to the East Coast to see family. Although I wouldn't fly with COVID raging, mid-March I checked airfares and found cheap tickets between Cedar Rapids and Newark, New Jersey. Now in April, I see only two flights a day on United's website, about $1000. No matches to Baltimore or Reagan in D.C.

When I work in the yard, I'm cheered by the whistles and lilting repetitions of birds, and the low hum of bumble bees, kind companions in a time of collective grief and not knowing. Our newly-married son is a paramedic in Maryland; his wife is an ER nurse. Our son-in-law is a firefighter in Baltimore where they don't give first responders PPE. I have aunts and uncles in Florida. New Jersey, my home state, has been hit hard; my brother there has lost two friends. Our family stays in touch more these days through texts and in Zoom and Hangouts.

Early on I was consumed with learning how to live now, and devising ways to care for loved ones near and far, even if just through warnings and prayer. That has quieted. We have enough food, toilet paper, homemade masks, hand sanitizer. My husband, a son who came to stay with us from California, and I have found our routines and spaces as we work peaceably from home.

I am transforming our wild yard into a tamer one, replacing the forest and field plantings of the previous owner with grass, as well as shrubs and flowers from a nursery. His plants have multiplied into a scraggly mass. For a while we kept it under control, before I entered graduate school and began to travel more.

This isn't regular gardening. It's a slow process to remove stubborn plants by pulling, digging out and covering large areas with brown landscaping cloth and cardboard sprinkled with a layer of mulch to smother what remains underneath. It's time and labor intensive, to avoid the potential harm of Round-up, the easier solution.

A small patch of purple meadow phlox stays and thrives in a corner. Dangling pink bleeding hearts seem more vivid from across our just-cleared backyard. I've put in purchased hydrangeas and coleus and moved hostas to new locales.

I believe I hear the birds more distinctly than before, along with chattering squirrels and breezes through branches. The environment feels less harried and cluttered from the government's shuttering and paring down. Maybe that's also true for my mind. I consider much among plants I don't know by name that I labor to remove. And my spirit breathes a prayer of gratitude for simple, blessed surprises in this time of crisis and unbidden sequestering.

Janet Skiff earned an MFA in Creative Nonfiction Writing from Vermont College of Fine Arts and often seeks to meld poetry and prose. She leads a writing workshop for former inmates returning to her community and lives in Iowa with her husband Fred and little-guy dog Nubbins.

DEEN FERRELL

❦

HELLO DARKNESS,
A VIEW FROM INSIDE THE WORLD OF
COVID-19

Words from the Simon & Garfunkel song play round in my head; "Hello darkness, my old friend; I've come to talk to you again." After sitting in my house for a week, having little human interaction beyond voices on a phone, watching detached heads bob in a sea of fuzzy color on my computer screen, a sort of darkness has set in. Words from the song do, as Paul Simon promises, *grow* in one's mind — like a cancer; like a plague.

Welcome to 2020. Welcome to our world of pandemic.

When I was a boy, I had a recurring nightmare that I woke up one day, and my house was empty. I walked through all the rooms calling, but no-one was there. I walked outside. There were birds. There were sounds of insects, but there were no people. As a teen, I recall cleaning a bank on the weekends. I stood in the middle of an intersection, looking out in all directions at an industrial part of the city completely abandoned on weekends. I stared, first one direction, then another, down long streets into a silent city, watching street lights change from red, to green, to red in their programmed cadence. But no cars stopped or started. No people busily shuffled their feet along the sidewalks or through the intersections. It was like a heart trying to pump, but there was no blood.

I go out for a jog sometimes in the mornings and face the same stillness; the same empty streets, and I feel the ghost of my young fears.

The horror of World Wars spread through the world like a darkness. It took shapes; German war machines belching smoke and fire; swastikas on raised arms as blonde boys shouted in unison. The villain in our pandemic, however, is too small to be seen. It crosses carefully laid front lines and invades the world of our thought as well as the physical form of our bodies. Like a destroying angel, it taps on the shoulder, taking one here, two there. Is it any wonder that some choose to shout? Blame is a game that excels in the dark.

How do we keep from getting forever lost?

I spent a summer once on the island of Lanai in Hawaii. With a total absence of artificial light in some areas of the island, I was fascinated how the skies came alive with lights beyond measure. Perhaps in embracing our darkness, we, too, can discover new sources of light. Could neighbors start to look out for neighbors, regardless of the color of their skin? Could nations put their bickering aside long enough to join in a common cause? Could humanity learn from this pandemic the importance of being better stewards, and students, of our planet?

I find myself more and more searching the dark of the times to find those few points of light. Glimmers of hope draw me, like a sunflower, to face turning to face new directions, to see new perspectives. On Facebook, on YouTube, in email, through text, I begin to find a sky vibrant with new light; souls that seem able to find their glow from within. While I pray in gratitude for all those fighting the disease, and fighting for a cure, there are so many more points of light out there. I only hope that to someone, somewhere, I can sparkle with a light of my own.

To my someone: You are loved. You are known. You are remembered. There are eyes that see beyond seeing; ears that hear beyond hearing; hearts that know what only hearts can know. The best of who we are will always survive, even through the darkest days. The long night will end. The sun is just beyond the horizon.

You will see it, and you will say; *hello light, my good friend! Let us sit and talk again...*

Deen Ferrell is an award-winning, Amazon Bestselling author. He has just released the fourth book in his Cryptic Spaces *series and will be releasing a children's book collaboration with Disney animator, Thomas Leavitt, within the next few months. He writes to inspire and provide hope while entertaining with his stories.*

MAGGIE ROSE

SADNESS OF A TREE

I was very fortunate to grow up exploring deep woods and waterways when I wasn't in school. I also took every opportunity to visit NYC as I became an adult. The art intrigued me - all of it - but the people intrigued me even more, along with astounding and terrifying me so much that I became a computer programmer. That part of me has never changed. No matter where I live, I seek peace in whatever nature is nearby. It is only in recent years that I have had the opportunity to learn to paint and tinker with robotics. The pandemic has provided a period of reflection that I needed. Thanks to time I am painting more, appreciating nature again, and grieving. To me, the creative process is a grieving process. We think and work to encapsulate truth or beauty. We want certain moments, experiences and discoveries recorded so that we can revisit them when we need to.

Sadness of a Tree, by Maggie Rose

FREDDIE MARTIN ARBUTHNOT

A POSITIVE LOOK

Goodness gracious, sakes alive, about three weeks into the pandemic and I was letting age, and the fact that I had no control of the circumstances, completely define me. I must take charge and make me as good as I could be!

I was born in 1934 and I lived through lots of adversity, and if you know me well, you know that I am a problem solver and a connector. If you have a problem, I will help you solve it, or I will connect you to someone who can help. So, if you don't want your problem solved, and you like having some excuse for your unhappiness, don't come to me. I am like a CSI or an investigator. In chemistry lab in college, I had to imagine that my material sample had to be the part of a murder scene that needed to be identified, made labs much more fun.

When COVID-19 appeared, I saw it as a challenge and immediately thought I should be wearing a mask. I visualized those little glitter particles being blown toward me trying to reach my respiratory system. Staying home was not a problem, because I have daughters who want to help me with anything I can't do with my computer connections. Just want to say that I am so grateful to be privileged to live in this electronic age. It is the greatest!

I live in the county on a few acres with eight rescued dogs, a very friendly cat, three little rescued dwarf goats and plenty of fresh air and sunshine. Some problems are really easy to solve, PLUG it in!

So many arguments about how COVID-19 got started: mean people in a lab, 5G, pollution, and about a million more. That's not the immediate problem to solve. The immediate problem is making your life better every day.

My solution:

Make my life as easy and productive as possible. This is a goal that I am always trying to reach.

Make my wellness top notch. As a holistic wellness coach and retired registered nurse, this is not a problem.

Have a great positive attitude.

Do everything possible to make my environment as pure as possible. I am an old farm girl and really care for it.

Help others make their lives great. I have learned that most people want to make their lives great, they want someone to do it for them.

My mission is contained in an old hymn, "What have I done in this world today, to help some on his way". You can find this hymn on your computer. I am frequently saying; "Alexa!" "What does this do", or, "What's the weather". I use Google several times a day and usually use the little microphones.

When COVID-19 first began, I became a bit lethargic and had a bad attitude for about two weeks, then I woke myself! I don't like time wasters, so I have a problem. As I have said, I am a problem solver – so let us solve the problem!

I am a lifelong learner, a widow that raised 4 children and I am very stubborn. So what an opportunity, right in front of me. Everyone wants time and I now have lots of TIME. 85 years of age is not old and I am well, the only person that I know who has only used my Medicare card once; on an eye injury. As a retired Registered nurse, I know lots of medical people but only trust me for my care. Last year I used a process and lots of supplements to remove my cataracts. I continue to do daily eye care. I don't like plastic and didn't want a plastic lens.

I need to help others via phone and email.

I have lots of books that need to be read, most on my Kindle.

I need to develop a top-notch wellness program.

I need to put together a daily learning program, researching and leading three to five hours a day. A great helper is the ability to transfer information from my tablet to the TV.

Build my exercise into my chores on my little farm and animal care.

I keep a journal and will relate what a page is like. One reason I keep busy; I hate housework, so if I am busy, I don't have time for housework.

The most important things I do:

Think good thoughts, go barefoot (I am always barefoot), laugh and play every day, accomplish something every day and pat myself on my back. The child in me needs lots of praise for a job well done.

My yard has a 'Mema corner' where I can do my rebounding and meditation every morning and every afternoon. I have an indoor nest with everything I need within my reach. In my outdoor space I am very content, and love to spend lots of time there when weather permits.

My social security check is small so my daughters help me and I do things for them.

Here is a sample of a day in Mema's life…

• Blood pressure 115/59, pulse 74, oxygen level 94%.

• Morning greeting to all the animals and my little farmette

- Goat care and walk with Mema and the animals to a meeting place in the yard for rebounding and meditation. I also give the animals treats in Mema's corner.
- Dog and cat care and feeding
- Eye care and early supplements, six capsules and six liquids.
- Banana and mushroom/adaptations coffee
- Lessons:
- About an hour on microbiome and food
- Positive attitude and new book review
- New information on anti-aging supplements
- Take the other supplements I need, twelve caps.
- Midday run with animals, do some mowing if it is not too hot.
- Phone and emails connections.
- Etc. Etc.
- And so the day goes. If there is some down time I can play Wordscapes or read a book.
- Most important is to laugh and play every day.

My life has been rich and full with family, lofty animals and love of God's earth. Holistic wellness advocate and retired registered nurse. Have had many occupations.

ROSHMI ROY

ISOLATION DURING LOCKDOWN: THE SILVER LINING

Isolation is a word we are all familiar with right now, in its various forms and connotations. In COVID times everyone has experienced isolation – from friends, from family members who are far away, from colleagues at the workplace you are no longer required to attend. The lockdown caught us unawares, and we were faced with unforeseen situations. Along with mobility restrictions, there was fear and anxiety – fear of being in the isolation ward of the hospital.

As a senior citizen who lives alone, following lockdown directives meant not leaving the house for any reason other than buying groceries or medicines. Since I am a believer in self-reliance, which is reliance on one's own efforts and abilities, I never have the need for household help. So, the absence of maids did not hit me like it did most Indian housewives.

Forced isolation has many repercussions. Man, being a social animal, thrives on relationships with others. Hence, isolation from the rest of society creates a sense of loss. We are dependent on others for reassurance of our self-worth. Emotional and social isolation can lead to feelings of anxiety and emptiness. Also, social isolation and loneliness can have adverse effects on health.

However, there are some who enjoy being alone, which is not the same thing as being lonely. Being alone is not having friends or family around you. Loneliness is the feeling of not having any meaningful relationship or interactions. You may feel lonely in the middle of a party if you cannot connect with anyone. 'Lonely' is associated with sadness, when you have a feeling of abandonment.

On the other hand, even when you are physically alone, you may be perfectly happy. Some people can be happy in their own company, and have no need of others to feel complete. I am lucky that I belong to this category. I enjoy my own company. It is an emotional state when you feel complete without the need for companionship. To quote from Jean Paul Sartre, "If you are lonely when you're alone you are in bad company."

Although accepting 'social distancing' as the 'new normal' may seem difficult to some, the concept of maintaining a distance from others has been around for some time. Many people voluntarily choose to become a recluse or a hermit and stay away from 'the madding crowd'.

Henry David Thoreau chose to distance himself from society and went to live in a cabin he built near Walden Pond as an experiment in self-sufficiency. It was also an exercise in simple living and spiritual self-discovery.

Think of solitude is a gift. It gives time for introspection, for delving into your inner being and discovering truths. It is why sages chose the depths of the forest or a cave in the mountains to isolate themselves in their search for spiritual growth.

So, the silver lining is that isolation is a boon, a time for regeneration and new awakenings, a time to discover the joys of simple and self-reliant living, of distancing ourselves from the mad rush of the consumerist world. You must know how to make the most of it. Be grateful for this time that has been given to us.

*After a successful career as a professor of English and Business Communication, Roshmi Roy is now engaged in imparting knowledge on Soft Skills and Personality Development, and has recently published a motivational book-*Climbing the Beanstalk: It's Up to You to Reach the Top.

CANDACE ARMSTRONG

OPEN-HEARTED

After ten days of quarantine, I talk to my houseplants, one by one. Soon, I give them names and imagined attributes. Their personalities surface. It is clear they like the attention and don't mind when I sing to them.

As the days warm, I move outside, gardening with intention, creating new beds and replanting old ones. I discover gardening centers are open and frequent them in full disguise: old gardening clothes, sunglasses, hat and mask. Digging, raking, mulching and watering leaves me dirty, sweaty and beset with new aches and pains. But, too tired and happy to worry about COVID-19.

Now as summer reaches its apex, I have new fears to overcome. My country is on fire, literally and figuratively, and my belly feels like it's full of hot coals every time I watch the news. Blooms of spring wilt. I simply cannot wrap my mind around the cruelty and patent disregard for the very existence of other people, let alone their rights. Yet their rights are my rights, and the indignity of losing them insults me down to my muddy shoes. It is a confusion of power.

History tells us when the powerless unite and rise up en masse, they prevail. How about a little respect? The mighty wielding implements of control shall someday be weak. Their days might be coming soon, at least for this time in this early century. Still the suffering and injustice rages on or reappears in another guise. Perhaps, as some say, this is the way of humanity but that doesn't make it acceptable.

The overall view calls for cultivating better relationships and limiting the spread of an invasive species. Some things are simpler to say than to do. Confronted with reality, we seek refuge but there is no escape from the real work that needs to be done.

What to do? I write letters, make modest donations, stay informed and aware, speak truth as I know it when I can and pray – because I do believe in a Higher Power.

Returning to my garden, I plant Blue Coneflower (Centaurea cyanus) for hope and tend the Peace Lily (Spathaphylum) summering outside in the shade. This fall I will plant Daffodil bulbs for New Beginnings to bloom in the spring.

Candace Armstrong writes in the beautiful woodlands of Southern Illinois. Her work has been published both in print and online. She spends more time writing, gardening and hiking than updating her website which is a work-in-progress.

MARY ANNE ANDERSON

BEFORE THE AFTER

Before awareness, the waters knew,
their tides swelled a slow stirring
undertow, underfoot
while we frolicked and splashed
floating weightless on the shores of oblivion.

Before awakeness, the wind retreated,
held its breath,
gasped,
then let out a single sorry sigh,
spewing dust and time-drenched molecules
the perfect storm.

Before aliveness, the soul journeyed
the earth and beyond,
knew its purpose:
to survive, to thrive, to do no harm
then become immortal.

Before sickness, germs gathered,
united soldiers of revenge,
as of to say
You fools, you silly selfish lot
while we carried on

met face to face
as they sprinkled their poison like fairy dust.

Before darkness spread its velvet blanket
over us like a shroud,
peeled off the color from our faces,
white blindness struck like a lighting bolt
thrust us toward the burning sun.

Dear Human Race
Mother Earth here.
I've been trying to reach you
for the longest time.
You do realize that I birthed you
and care for you.

Why can't you behave like good children?
Do I have to remind you again and again
to wash off that soot?

And please stop bickering over
who gets the most goodies.
The trees
the oils and minerals
the food supplies
are for all of you to share.
Please kids
pick up your litter.
And clean up your rooms for heaven's sake.

You act as if you don't care.
Really?
This time you'll be sorry.

You'll regret soiling me so badly
I can't ever get rid of the stains.
And the way you've cut off my air supply,
shame on you!
You kids deserve a good spanking
Maybe I should flood you with my tears again.
Or give you a good shaking.
Goodness knows I've tried to warn you.

Go ahead,
keep pummeling me with your drills,
burden me with too much weight,
burn away the hair on my skin.
You can't run and you can't hide.
You'll pay for this,
my undeserving progeny.

I can wipe you out with a single sneeze.
Better yet
let a rogue germ do it for me.
I'll just sit back and watch you perish.
I can always make other children,
ones more deserving of my bounty.

Unless. . . unless. . .
hmmm
let me think.

Okay
go to your rooms,
cover your faces in shame.
Isolation.
That ought to do it for now.

This is your last warning.

Sincerely,
Gaia

THE MIRROR HAS TWO FACES

The Way I Feel It:

It's hard to sleep.
Dark dreams with their
continual loop
would baffle even the absurdists.

Dreams beyond imaging
that cast me down the rabbit hole
repeat
then repeat backwards.

Here they come again
in my waking hours
like gargoyles licking their lips
hungry for the taste of
blood and fear.

The Way You Cope:

You sink into dreamless sleep
no motion
only quiet breaths
soft like the blush of sunrise.

The moon hides behind the dawn
no comfort required.
A bright new day awaits
with blurred periphery.

Breakfast as usual.
Sameness sedates you
routine your escape hatch.
You write down "strawberries"
on the yellow note pad.

I am a poet/singer/lyricist/author whose appreciation for Art and Life are intertwined with threads of humanity and compassion. I've published in numerous places and have won several awards, but that's not my main motivation. Love and Light are my wings.

JIM FITZGERALD

❧

THE POWER OF NATURE

The early 2020 lockdown due to the COVID-19 has been a difficult time for all of us. It is a personal and financial strain, on multiple levels, to almost everyone on the planet. It is especially frustrating because, as with the long-ago indeterminate prison sentences, there is no definitive end date to its blight upon the human race. Those sentences have since been ruled unconstitutional, but no such abolition can be readily applied to the invisible enemy known as the Coronavirus. Not yet, anyway.

It lives among us and is killing us on a daily basis. It is scary. My present means of coping, my present means of maintaining my sanity, has been to immerse myself in the finer elements of life that sometimes go unobserved whilst leading our 'normal', everyday existence.

That includes the sound of birds chirping, the pitter-patter of a rain storm, the power of the blowing wind, and the colorful tapestry of the setting sun. Yes, the dynamic vibrancy of nature as it emerges in the early spring has helped me keep some semblance of the routine during these troubling times. It's not lost on me that nature, in the form of this cursed virus, is the cause of these problems. However, appreciating nature, in all its glory, is also a means to escape its constant reality.

In closing, I will never perceive mother nature the same way as before. It is a force to reckon with, both positively and negatively. I do my best to focus on the former.

Jim "Fitz" Fitzgerald remains an active criminal profiler and forensic linguist. He spent 20 years in the FBI as a Supervisory Special Agent, along with 11 years before that as a police officer/detective/sergeant on the Bensalem Twp. (PA) PD. During his extensive and varied law enforcement career he successfully investigated numerous homicides, sexual assaults, kidnappings, bank robberies, and other violent crimes, as well as matters of international notoriety to include the Unabomber, Jon Benet Ramsey, Anthrax, and DC Sniper cases as a profiler and/or a forensic linguist.

JOLI ANGEL ROBINSON

TIME FOR A RESET

In this age of COVID many of us have experienced a gamut of emotions. Some days are better than others. Many of us have had to learn how to live life differently from how we have ever experienced it or known it to be. The sadness of watching millions of people die here in the United States due to the Coronavirus and its complications, while also experiencing loss of jobs and a looming eviction crisis is more than many of us can stomach at this time. Many of us are also experiencing incredible trauma not only dealing with the impact of COVID-19, but witnessing the continued deaths of Black men and women by police, the continued assaults and murders of Black Transgender women, and what feels to be an increasingly venomous hate growing within the borders of our country. 2020 has been a tough year to handle.

Through the immense growing pains of 2020, COVID-19 has also brought about a renewed energy of discovering creative ways to enjoy our homes, find our peace, and cherish our families. There has been a movement to reconnect with hobbies and pick up old pastimes that our pre-COVID lives never seemed to have enough time for. I have gained a new sense of what is important to me and the busy, hurried life of jam-packed community events and involvement is not necessarily how I want to continue to spend the rest of my days. Without the pause and the reset that COVID-19 has brought to my life, I would have possibly never come to this revelation. The initial struggle to figure out a new normal was replaced with an appreciation for a simpler, less hectic life and schedule. At times, there was literally nowhere else to be than at home.

To be fair, I am an eternal optimist. I can find the tiniest sliver of silver-lining in any rain cloud. And when I crawled out of the muck of how horrible this time in our history feels and the desire to just throw all of 2020 away, I found a beauty in having and taking the time to walk in the park or snuggle up with a good book, instead of spending that time scheduling meetings and adding additional projects to my calendar.

I have also determined that I never want to go back to the unnatural way that I packed my every waking hour with something I deemed productive. That constant need to fill my time did not give me room to focus on nourishing my spirit or fully taking care of my emotional needs. I have found joy in simple things like picking random movies and watching ridiculous TV show series, like *Tiger King*. This has felt like the hard reset that I did not even realize that my life needed. I am enjoying the slower pace of my evenings. I have picked back up my love for cooking and I have thoroughly enjoyed learning new cocktail recipes, one of which I snagged from a Martha Stewart magazine (I strongly suggest you try her Rose Sangria with Nectarines and Strawberries recipe). I have perfected the art of enjoying my own space, filling it with those things that I love, and allowing the moment of absolute nothingness to not fill me with anxiety. I have passionately embraced the understanding that my body and mind need rest. This hard reset has been a surprisingly good reminder of those things that are truly important to me and have forced me to wrestle with the busyness and imbalanced priorities I previously let lead my life.

I have learned that there is no magic pot of gold at the end of an imaginary rainbow that I must go on a mad dash to find before anyone else. I have learned to embrace and enjoy the peace and quiet and stillness thrust upon me by COVID-19. And I have fully realized the unnecessary distractions that kept me in what now feels like an unsustainable hamster wheel race.

Surprisingly, COVID-19 has been a great time for me to focus on aligning and balancing and resetting my life and intentions and goals. I hurt for those that have felt the tremendous blow that Coronavirus has given to their lives. I pray for our healthcare workers who have truly been on the frontlines of this pandemic. I am grateful for those who have been in the trenches of addressing the ravaging impact of this massive health crisis. I also have gained a greater appreciation for how this time has allowed me a moment to sit, rest, and catch my breath. I've missed me.

Joli Angel Robinson manages Community Engagement efforts for the Dallas Police Department. She also serves as a Co-Chair for the Dallas Truth, Racial Healing, & Transformation organization. Joli is currently working on her doctorate from the University of Southern California in Organizational Change and Leadership.

CAROLINE COLLINS

A CANTICLE FOR THE EARTH IN A
TIME OF QUARANTINE

Praise God for new tourists,
those goats massed outside churches,
feasting on hedges, that family of boars crossing
against the light, the sheep milling
around an empty McDonald's.
Praise God for the all-day splash of mallards
in the fountain at Trafalgar Square,
for geese blatting away on the airport tarmac.
Praise God for bald eagles
piling so many nests in saguaros,
for leatherbacks flippering
across lonely beaches,
for all those returning to places
long writ in their bones.
Praise God for the splendor
coming to life, ribbons of mountains
now coming clear, trees breaking into bloom
after so many barren years.
Praise God for wild solitude, for langurs
who frolic on sidewalks,
for pandas who find each other again
in sudden ardor, for lions
who slumber through the afternoons

by quiet roads. Praise God
for the earth, blossoming
gloriously in our absence, so full
of the goodness that is the Lord's.

Caroline Collins teaches college-level composition, creative writing, and American literature. Her collection of poetry, Presences, *was published by Parallel Press in 2014.*

ACTS OF KINDNESS

Nichelle Taylor

All Write: A Story of the Virtual Writing Community

April 2020 was the coldest, harshest Spring I had ever experienced in my eighteen years in Colorado, but it was not just the slushy snow piled up on the streets or the incessant, bitter wind that bothered me. Winter hung around for a while, allowing a chill that bore into my bones to sneak in under doors and through fuzzy pajamas.

The brumal cold came in through the news, images of loved ones dying alone in hospitals, close-knit communities distancing themselves from one another. Weeks of no makeup, no shaving, days gone without washing my hair.

I was a full-time student and a part-time employee wrapping up my fourth semester of university all online, dealing with new deadlines and projects that came in a sea of sticky notes that domineered my planner, and spending my days on Zoom for both classes and work. Chained to my desk in the freezing basement, I managed crushing migraines and frozen, stiff fingers, reaching for blankets that made me feel heavier instead of warmer. On top of it all, I felt lost in my writing pursuit.

I decided to become an author about the time I hit puberty, and ever since, I had always been working on a story. In the months prior to the pandemic, I had finished writing a novel and began querying for literary agents, but as the quarantine forced time to blur, rejection emails started coming faster and faster, and my motivation only appeared in sporadic moments between Zoom meetings.

Caught in a creativity rut, the place where everything sat still, I wondered how I could continue my writing endeavor as I spent my little free time recharging from hours of staring at the computer. How could I bust out a novel like I saw others doing when I had so much else to do?

Hoping to ignite some creative spark, I passed my time reading *The Stand* by Stephen King, praying that the conspiracy theories on Twitter were not prophetic, and scrolling through Instagram. I noted all the friendly faces that stuck out, preaching about self-care and nurturing one's creative side during the pandemic. Goal-setting. I had always prided myself on my ability to plan, but in debilitating times where no one could be in control, I was losing that aspect of myself, too.

Finally, I found whispers of something I had never heard about over on Instagram, called NaNoWriMo, short for National Novel Writing Month. In April and July each year, the site holds a "Camp NaNoWriMo" to practice for November, when everyone attempts to write 50,000 words in a month. When I realized what a cool opportunity this would be, I took to a post and asked, "I'm considering trying Camp NaNoWriMo. What do you all think?"

I was overwhelmed by all the encouraging responses, promising me it would be worth it, that the experience was very fulfilling, and that they would be with me every step of the way. Indeed, they were.

I posted weekly updates of my new work in progress, a Young Adult Fantasy novel I had only dreamed up a short time before. Weird for me, someone who feeds from planners and mind-boggling details. I guess the spontaneity of the year was contagious.

For the entire month of April, I awoke early before work and classes to get in a daily word count. I had set my goal for 30,000 words, and my virtual cheerleaders kept me going. Along the way, I developed new friendships that took me completely by surprise.

While I was isolated from the rest of the world, I found a whole community of book lovers and dreamers to help me succeed in my goal. After Camp NaNoWriMo was over, I found that I had written 32,000 words, the most I had ever written in such a short amount of time. My goal-setting mojo had been restored, and I finally found faith in my creativity again.

Even though the word count was a huge accomplishment for me, what left me feeling even prouder was the endless support, the community I saw between scrolls and double-tapped likes.

I had never imagined that social media would provide me a meaningful support group, but in the writing community, it is clear everyone only wants each other to succeed. It was during my time on Instagram that I was able to create these new friendships that I have kept up in the months since.

As May came to Colorado, the frigid air lingered, but I felt better about my accomplishments. I finished my online semester with straight A's and reclaimed my passion for writing.

With a cup of hot tea in hand, I looked out the window at the falling snow, and as I remembered those who were struggling out there in our world, those who continued to fight for their health and their own communities, I felt grateful for the one I found within my phone.

I would never have believed I could find such a wonderful community online, but thanks to the wonderful Bookstagrammers, aspiring authors, and the kindness they bestowed upon me, I was able to write my heart out, finishing that Young Adult Fantasy novel at 85,333 words at the end of June 2020. The virtual writing community has continued to cheer me on, and because of them, my story of isolation ended up being all right.

Nichelle Taylor is a 20-year-old aspiring author from Colorado. Her work has appeared in the University of Northern Colorado's literary magazine, The Crucible, *and she received an Honorable Mention for her short story, "The Monstrous Form" in the Writer's Digest 88th Annual Writing Competition.*

JET TORRES

SILVER LININGS

I have learned. I have learned about my strengths and weaknesses. Most importantly, I have learned to accept acts of kindness when kindness is offered. I am a proud disabled Veteran with a Down Syndrome child. The past four years have been riddled with sadness, challenges and extreme exhaustion.

When the coronavirus occurred, my daughter had just survived her sixth surgery. At three years old, she showed more resilience than I have shown the entire 41 years of my existence. I knew that I needed to be strong enough for her and for myself. Weak minds, hearts and resolve have no place in raising a special needs child – especially, with a military injury that could either be my downfall or stepping stone into a new way of existence.

As a single parent of a special needs child, I thought my options at normalcy were dwindling. I felt depression trying to elbow its way into my happy realm. Working a part-time job at Home Depot brought on doubts about how we would continue to survive. Where was the silver lining? The first act of kindness came from my Home Depot colleagues. They made a generous financial donation. That small act of kindness was enough to bolster my efforts to keep us ahead of poverty and heartache.

Refusing to feel sorry for myself, I decided I would take a stand against giving up. After all, there was a little angel and a sweet canine depending on me. They did more than make me smile – they absolutely tickled my soul.

I emailed my resume to our local Veteran Services office. There were certain programs I could not qualify for, because of my daughter's disability. The second act of kindness came from a Veteran Representative I spoke with, who took a personal interest in our story. He realized my corporate experience would be a great asset to any organization. He and his wife joined forces and emailed my resume to all their contacts who could possibly assist.

The third act of kindness came from an employer who was willing to take me into their fold. The employer is a woman-owned business, with award-winning accolades for hiring military veterans. They were quick to put my skills to use, in what can be described as a mutually beneficial relationship.

We were amongst the first to self-quarantine, back in March 2020. My daughter's lung disease was reason enough to seek alternate work arrangements. My employer was understanding and approved the new telecommute schedule. At the time, I was still researching the dangers associated with Coronavirus, but inherently knew our lives would be forever changed (again). It was up to us to navigate how the pandemic would shape our future. We could either cower in self-pity, or start roaring like a lion.

Right around this time, I met an American Legion representative, who wanted to know more about our little family's trials and tribulations. I seized the moment and began to get involved with our local post, searching for ways I could immediately give back to our community. I volunteered as a marketing and social media consultant, to quickly communicate CDC-approved information and protect veterans from false Coronavirus details.

The fourth act of kindness was from the same American Legion post, who volunteered to drop off food so that my daughter and I could avoid crowded grocery stores. Many of the curbside and pick-up services were backlogged, leaving high-risk families vulnerable. I began to be an advocate, reaching out to our Chamber of Commerce, and inquiring about contact-free food donations.

Because I swallowed pride and reached out for help, I have been able to focus more of my attention on our daughter's physical, educational and emotional development. We have taken advantage of American Sign Language (ASL) tutorials, IEP instruction, speech therapy, and online educational activities. Most of all, I get to experience cuddles throughout the day.

There have been so many acts of kindness along the way, even since these experiences. Now, I do not ask where the silver lining is but rather how can I be somebody's silver lining today, tomorrow and beyond? How can I help the Down Syndrome and veteran community – a special niche if there ever was one! If we are all in this together, then count me in to shine a light on our citizens who need a little extra effort and support.

JET Torres is a Disabled Army Veteran with a Down Syndrome child and a clever Shih-Tzu. Together, we make a heck of a team! Passion comes in all different shapes, colors and breeds.

JET Torres and her daughter
© 2020 Violetta Markelou

MAURIZIO BIANCARDO

THE GLASS HALF FULL

In the near distance the church bells chime out their rejoicing message Resurrection and new hope.

There are many amongst us because of the challenging deceptions of life, who may have become mute to such echoing messages.

Just like many of us may look at our lives seeing constantly the glass half empty.

Those who are positive and optimistic will say: "The glass is half full."

Others may say: "It does not matter whether the glass is half full or empty, the point you are missing is the glass is refillable."

Challenges, deception, hurt and sadness come to us all. Just like Faith, love, happiness and joy.

So as the chiming bells of Easter slow down and then stop until another year, let us not forget to search for something positive in each day.

Even if some days we have to search harder than others.

Let us remember that every storm that comes, also comes to an end.

Let us become the rainbow in somebody else's life.

Remind those who have fallen weak, that difficult roads often lead to beautiful destinations.

Guide the lost and hopeless towards the sun, making sure the shadows fall only behind them.

Remind ourselves and others that life is 10% of what happens to us and 90% of how we deal with it.

Let us not forget that obstacles are just simply stepping stones helping us reach our goals.

And for those who have lost faith. Despite their colour, creed, religion or faith...

Remind them that one of Earth's saddest days and gladdest days were just three days apart.

And as for the glass...

We must be grateful we have a glass and that there is something in it.

Or better yet. With our glass half full or empty. Let us seek out those who are thirsty and share...

Raised by an immigrant Italian Family in the North of England, life has brought me many difficult challenges but I have always tried to look at life with the glass half full.

RIDDHI SARKAR

WHO WILL YOU BE?

The times were endless when my instincts steered me in the direction of looking at the real picture of the world. The persistent questions that came up were always about "Who we are?" and "What are we doing?"

Even though the voice inside always guided me towards what needed to be done to help others and myself, I was often clouded by judgements and feelings of getting hurt. All these stipulations had put me in societal shackles which seemed unbreakable, until the year 2020.

When the entire world was battling with the havoc-causing virus, I was fighting with a virus of my own. A virus that slowly infests your soul and makes you vulnerable to any thought, incident, people, events around that do not serve you for your own good.

What is a virus?

In medical terms, it is an interactive agent that disrupts certain functionalities of your physical body, hence making you fall sick.

In technological terms, it is a program, which when executed in your operating system, makes your computer go all wonky.

In spiritual terms, it is a soul-crushing negative vibe or feeling which often takes over your happiness and successfully leads you towards the path of depression, anxiety and much more.

Now the question is, what does a virus do? It may come in our lives in numerous forms or perspectives as I call them, but their sole and whole intention is always to honor the rule that nature follows which is 'survival of the fittest'.

Why do we look at it as something bad? Why do we not look at it as one of the teachers who come in our vicinity to teach us how to respect what we have been given and enjoy it at the same time?

This year was chalked out to be the best year of my life, as I thought I had finally put together pieces of certain puzzles which felt imminent at that time. But now if I look at it, those puzzles were never mine in the first place. They were bestowed on me by social pressures, expectations, the need to prove something to certain people and so on.

But as soon as the year started, the virus infected us all in one way or another. When we were locked in our houses, it taught us to respect the freedom that we have and not take it for granted, it taught us to check upon one another and not just pretend to be there, it taught us patience as we waited in long lines to get access to our daily needs and wants, it taught us the value of certain things as we lost touch with most of our necessities for a long period of time, like it taught me tolerance.

It taught me that I did not have to follow all those rules and beliefs. It taught me to break free from those bonds that were made up by society to keep all under control. It showed me the real faces of certain family members who called me whenever something was needed, but never picked up their phone to check on me even once during the pandemic. And that is when I realized that the virus does not care if you live in a First World developed country or a Third World growing country, it does not care if you live in the slums or in the condos high up, it treats you exactly the same when it knocks on your door.

It will either break you or make you, depending on how strong you are to understand and work along with it.

Tolerance is easier said than done. To be tolerant of something you need to be near that feeling, person, thing, or event that you are intolerant of. Only then can you look yourself in the mirror and say, "I think I do not like this, but I can learn how to be tolerant of this, instead of acting out."

The period of the pandemic affected my best friend in a different way. It took away his job, made him go through depression, gave him another better job, only to show him the faces of reality, then took that away too. But the day he started acting like a different person, saying things which he would never usually say, it made me get up and leave him behind.

I ran away, only to realise that not everything makes sense in the beginning, you do not always have to have it in the first go. You must learn to become tolerant of any situation that bothers you, instead of judging it. Only then you can find the solution and work towards it, because intolerance is a mirror that shows us a dissimilar image of ourselves.

The coronavirus took away a lot from us, but also gave us a lot in return. You can look deeper into your experiences and find that out yourselves. The virus showed us a different path of surviving; where unity, love, care, and bond should walk side by side. Only then can we evolve, only then can we be free from the vicious cycle of what is right or wrong, which will uplift the veil of blindness that we have all around the world, where injustice, greed, poverty, pain is inflicted on our fellow brothers and sisters, mothers and fathers, sons and daughters.

The year 2020 has given us a chance to let go and move forward, it has given us a chance to discover the universal truth which is belonging and acting as one mind and soul. Because when you think of everyone as your own, you do not inflict any harm, but shower only love and affection. If I could find my path that got lost among the expected bigotries of the world and my own self, so can you, which brings us to the question of: "Who will you be?"

Kindness, Compassion and Love, I vibrate with these three.

Debra Heirs

℗

Little Earthquakes

Utah. Zagreb.
The earth splits open,
crumbles stone buildings.
We are clueless in our big shoes.
The earth shakes under our weight.

Little earthquakes are happening all the time,
some are bigger than others. We only think
we are on solid ground, but the ground
is constantly shifting underneath us.

Meanwhile, the coronavirus known as COVID-19
rips at our lungs, without bias for a country's borders.

In every part of the world cities are shut down.
Suddenly the skies clear.
Someone on a balcony begins to sing.

Shelves are emptied at the supermarkets.
No toilet paper, no hand sanitizer, no disinfectant wipes,
meat and canned goods are in short supply.
Neighbors post alerts on social media:
There was a delivery, Tuesday 11 a.m.
It's gone in a few hours.

How much do we really need?

Meanwhile, the virus spreads.
The death count is rising.
Everyday heroes keep showing up.

What can we do?
We can be kind to one another.

Our own innate goodness is still here,
humming along in the cracks, at the ready.
Catch it. Hold it. Pass it on.
You can't put a price tag on what doesn't expire.

Debra Hiers is a poet deeply influenced by Buddhism, our connection to the
natural world, and the healing power of poetry. She is an improvisational
musician and combines playful clarinet musings with her poetry in
presentation. Debra currently resides in Atlanta, GA.

JoAnne Bennett

Lead With Your Heart

Back during the start of the pandemic, I called the rehabilitation center just down the street from my home to see if they might have some residents who would like a few of the adult coloring care packages that I had put together. Mr. Nice Guy, John, who answered the phone said he thought that they could find a couple of interested patients. John assured me that they would take the necessary steps to keep the coloring books in quarantine for an appropriate amount of time as a cautionary measure. I then asked him if he was going to be there for a little while, because I would just leave the coloring books and markers right outside their front entrance.

"Almost all night," he answered.

Well, if you know me, I couldn't leave him out, especially when we are honoring and celebrating the 'heroes' who are taking such good care of our loved ones and the most vulnerable. I told him he could also have a coloring book if he would like one, but Mr. Nice Guy said he was good. At the end of our brief conversation and his comment about how nice it was of me to do this, he asked, "Do you have a name?" Sometimes I do, but other times it is just not all that important. My name is JoAnne.

Less than a week later, when I drove by the same rehab center, I saw an older woman sitting in a wheelchair close to the window. She seemed so sad and lonely. I wanted to get out of my car and pretend that I was a young girl again waving and smiling at her from afar. Or even leave some beautiful flowers outside the door for her. It's hard to imagine what those who are being quarantined (away from their homes) must be going through without their support systems. I hope this pandemic doesn't feel like it's going to last forever for this woman. I sent her a gentle hug.

Sometimes, I can so clearly see it is a God-thing. Over a month later, I stopped by the rehab center with a bouquet of flowers for the sad-looking woman. The same nurse, Mr. Nice Guy, met me outside (we were standing six feet apart and wearing masks) and I handed him the flowers. He said, "You are bringing these for her and you're not even a relative? Would you like to meet her?" He brought her to the window so we could wave at each other. She told him I could be her daughter, and thanked me.

I drove by the rehab place again recently. I haven't seen my new elderly friend sitting by the window in her wheelchair lately. I've been hoping that she is okay. I have heard sirens a lot in recent days close by and wondered if they were for her. But then, I saw such a sweet sight this afternoon. I don't know if it was my new friend on the other side of the glass door or not, but this animated guy was on his knees with his hands placed on the glass obviously communicating with someone in a wheelchair.

If I don't get to see this woman again, who said that I could be her daughter, I want her to know that she helped me as well. I want to thank her for letting me be her daughter for even just a few minutes. Sometimes, the void in our own hearts is filled by reaching out to others with caring and kindness.

The people who raised me were not generous, caring individuals, especially when it came to perfect strangers. My stepfather used to own a convalescent home. When I was a young girl, I remember coming up with this exciting idea all by myself. I asked my parents if I could take a lily on Easter Sunday to one of the patients. I was thankful that for once my parents did not try to stop me. On that special day, I experienced what I believe is most important in this world, compassion, selflessness, and love for others. Sometimes, it comes back to bless us in the most unexpected ways. It was that significant moment from my childhood which has clearly defined who I strive to be as an adult.

I love focusing on my passion – writing. As an author, my heart-felt desire is to reach and out and encourage others to never give up on discovering your gifts. My personal essays have appeared in print and several publications over the years. My favorite piece is about making a difference in the lives of young people in an anthology, Dear Wonderful You.

Judith Speizer Crandell

ᑫᕊ

My Beautiful Shopper

We needed oranges, half-and-half, bread, etcetera. A friend suggested Shipt, a shopping service. After registering, I was assigned next-day delivery from Weis market. My list was long, my patience short. As delivery was delayed, I took yogic breaths. After all, I wouldn't go hungry, had a table to eat at, a husband and pets to share sheltering-in, right? *Gratitude must overshadow impatience.*

I clapped and jumped up and down – the most exercise I had that day – when shopper Sue chose to fill our cart. Sue texted me, "One red pepper or two?" "Which gluten free cookies?" "Salted, Lightly Salted, Salt-free Peanuts?" Suddenly, lovely photos of grocery shelves floated onto my iPhone. When I couldn't read labels, Sue instructed me how to enlarge them.

In between food questions, I discovered Sue loved and rescued animals. I sent photos of mine. We were bonding!

She suggested half gallons of seltzer when there were no quarts. Chocolate-glazed doughnuts in addition to iced ones. Avocadoes, perhaps? Three or four plum tomatoes? Moving along via text, Sue was my new 'friend', though I had no idea what she looked and sounded like.

Then she told me she would also deliver our groceries. So from inside my garage, masked and gloved, I watched a smiling blond woman unload my groceries. From afar, we said, "Hi." "Thank you." "Be well."

151

"Be well," the new sign-off. To all the service workers risking their own health to help preserve mine, "Be well." Thank you, Sue, my beautiful shopper.

Having resided on both coasts and in between, Judith Speizer Crandell has happily landed in Milton, Delaware. Solitary walks along the Atlantic beaches soothe her soul. Sharing these with her husband, Bill, a fellow writer, and their rescue dog, Windsor, enliven her soul and fuels her creativity. During this time of the COVID Pandemic, she spends more time at home but still tries to touch the ocean when she can.

JEFFREY ESTRELLA

EVERYDAY HOPE

Let me begin this by saying that I am an essential worker
so during this pandemic I've gotten to see both the best and
worst humanity has to offer. I've been screamed at for not
having toilet paper in stock, and I've been thanked profusely
for doing my job. It's been a roller coaster of an experience
for me and there have been days that I struggle with seeing
the light.

Both of my parents are at high risk for complications due
to COVID-19. So, I am perpetually worried about that. At the
beginning my job seemed to be lagging behind every other
company in protecting its workers, while others were getting
plexiglass shields and pay raises we were told the plexiglass
was coming eventually and here's a one-time bonus....So I
was worried about that...

I am also a writer in my free time, but when the pandemic
really began taking off, I basically slipped into survival
mode. I went to work, I came home, I ate and I slept. I didn't
read, I didn't write, I didn't even get to see my fiancée for
several months! I was going through the motions of life and
hoping that once time passed we'd do what we were always
supposed to do and we'd beat the virus.

However, after months of hoping and waiting we didn't
seem to be getting closer to beating the virus and the
pandemic was dragging on, deaths were piling up, my job
had given us some protections, and then had taken most of

them away, and I was lost, confused, scared, and angry. This feeling of being completely without direction went on for a while. Honestly, I wasn't until July that I really started to get back to a modicum of normalcy

During those months I had only one thing that kept me moving, that kept me doing everything I needed to, to sluggishly move through the muck and the darkness and that was Hope. Now I would love to talk about this one big event that changed my thinking, this one big act of kindness that lit the path…but I think it was the little things. I got to celebrate eleven years with my fiancée, I got to celebrate accomplishments in writing, I got to talk with friends a little more, I saw people paying for supplies for mothers, fathers, sisters, brothers, people on the street. I watched as humanity came together to help those who needed it most, and those little things, the little kindnesses that I would have looked away from before the pandemic are the things that have gotten me through it.

One of those things that I had taken advantage of in the past was our local Relay For Life; which helps raise money for cancer research, and celebrate and remember the lives of those we've lost, or honor those fighting and surviving their own battles. This year due to COVID-19 our event would be a virtual event, which was a nice tribute on its own but nothing beats actually being there in person. A few days after that, we got an email stating that we were going to do a socially distanced in-person event so, in late June, my community got together and things looked a little differently. We were confined to our parking spaces, our cars decorated with our team's themes, our facemasks on, and despite the rain that was coming down and the pandemic, we celebrated the lives of those we've lost to cancer. We raised money for cancer research and cancer patients and families, and we walked a socially distanced lap around a track in silent remembrance of them, our path lit up by the luminaria bags that each carried the name of someone lost or someone still fighting. It was a night full of tears, laughter, solidarity, and most importantly love and hope.

If there is anything I've learned from this pandemic, it's to look for the little things. If you are feeling overwhelmed by the weight of the darkness, pay attention to the little kindnesses and use them to fuel your hope, and if you look around you and you can't seem to find any little kindnesses, make your own. Do something nice for somebody, pay for somebody's morning coffee, or let someone go in front of you in line at the store. Do something that will make you or somebody else smile and if you can do that, you'll feel that hope grow...

Now I'm not saying that the path out of this is easy, and that having experienced all this kindness that all the days of doubt and anger have magically gone away. There are days when the world still seems too much, and I feel myself getting angry or overwhelmed and feel myself slipping back into survival mode, but at least now I know what to look for and I truly believe that despite what we all see on the news or on social media, that humanity is good and that being hopeful isn't foolish. We are going through a lot of things and in such a short period that there are days where it seems certain that the world is going to end. I don't believe that. We will see the light at the end of the tunnel, we will beat this thing but it won't be in one big sweeping gesture. The way out of this is with a million little sacrifices and a million little kindnesses. Together we can make that change. It's something I only thought was true before the pandemic hit, but it's something I now know...

Jeffrey is a retail worker by day, writer, dreamer, optimist by night. He is hoping to spread hope by doing what he does best, telling stories.

MARGRET KINGREY

IN CELEBRATION OF THE MUNDANE

Do you spend your life surrounded by noise? Do you have a sense of desperation? Do you drive around feeling that you have never accomplished anything? Well, stop! Turn off the radio and the TV. Silence your cell phone, no matter how smart it is. Get out of your car and give yourself and your family a break. Do something simple, repetitive and mundane for at least one small stretch of time. Some say at least an hour, but I say try just five minutes to start. Five minutes will be hard enough to begin with for most of us.

First, listen to your own breathing. Feel your lungs fill with life-giving air. Sense the rise and fall of your chest, the air coming in through your nostrils, out through your mouth. This you can do anywhere, just connect with your own living breath. Most meditation exercises begin with breathing and no wonder. It is what keeps us alive. Don't try to change how you breathe, just be attuned to it.

Do you iron clothes? Most of my friends think I'm crazy to spend an hour a week ironing. Well, I use that time to get in touch with myself and pray for those who are close to me. I learn to be in the moment feeling the weight of the iron in my hand, letting my mind not worry about the future, what I am going to fix for dinner or the next client I will work with. It is important time to me. It isn't ironing so much as meditation and contemplation. Ironing allows the creative part of myself to feel free to be.

In *The Soul of the Chef,* Michael Ruhlman writes of the great chef, Thomas Keller. Keller was not born into a family that appreciated haute cuisine. He learned to take extreme care in the way he cleaned his kitchen and the way each dish was prepared, from the water he boiled to the chopping of ingredients. He even skinned the rabbits himself because he was very meticulous. The reverence with which he approached preparing food made him one of the renowned chefs of the time.

When you prepare your family meal or even one for yourself, do you do it with reverence to honor the people for whom you cook; or is it just a chore that has to be dispensed with as quickly as possible? The tasks needed to prepare a meal are mundane to be sure. Try this though, just once. Instead of buying those cute little carrots in a bag, make your own carrot sticks. Get a bag of unpeeled carrots. When you make carrot sticks for your child's lunch, or your own, peel each carrot with love for that person, lifting him or her up in thought as you slice the whole carrot into segments to put into a baggie. See if this doesn't give you a more loving attitude toward that person. Be intentional about wishing that person health and happiness as you prepare the carrot sticks. Don't say anything out loud. Just think your thoughts quietly and gently to yourself. It is especially important to not say anything to the person for whom you do this task. This act is not a tool for manipulating behavior of the child or adult for whom you prepare the carrot sticks. This is your unspoken offering to them to "have a good day". It is about your care and love for this particular individual. Don't have time to make carrot sticks? Try this while making the beds.

There are many small tasks that we can turn into reverential offerings to the people we love. These then become change agents for our attitudes toward what we do with our loved ones, not just for them.

Next, try baking cookies from scratch with members of your family. Teach the children to sift the flour, stir the shortening or butter into the dough, and clean up the mess when the baking is done. In going through the whole routine from beginning to end, we have time to talk, instruct and realize that such an activity creates memories which can sustain us for a lifetime. These are things children remember. They also learn that things take time and are worth spending time to do. These tasks are also worth the physical and mental effort to do.

The other wonderful thing about repetitive tasks is that they give us a chance to practice. If we are observant in how a thing is done each time we do it, we can get better at it. This builds skill. Children and some adults seem to feel that they need to do a thing perfectly the first time they do it. Well, no one ever does. Some things take more practice than others, and some things are more fun to practice than others, but frustration and boredom are a part of life and we all must learn to cope with them. Again, from *Soul of a Chef*, Keller states that he made hollandaise sauce every day for two years. He didn't just make the hollandaise, but tried each day to make it better than the day before. In order to do that he had to pay attention to what he did and how he did it, and adjust something each time. Isn't this what any student needs to do? We pay attention, don't rush and we make small adjustments as we practice in order to build skill. This is true for any skill we desire to know, or need to know. It is true for learning to tie our shoes, handwriting, painting a picture or playing soccer.

There was a saying in the Sixties that could be revised for today. It was, "Don't push the river. It flows by itself." Sometimes it seems that the more we try, the less we get done. This is when it is good to do something mundane. Do some gardening, bake bread, go for a walk – anything to just be with yourself for a while. Notice that the activities suggested have two primary components. They engage the physical body and they allow the thinking mind to rest. They don't require much thought, but they do require awareness of what is being done and the surroundings in which the activity takes place. It is important to focus on the activity. Do not think about getting it done and what you are going to do next.

Participating in the mundane allows the creative, intuitive aspects of ourselves to operate and bubble to the surface. We can use these insights for problem solving, creative activities and enhancing our spiritual growth. Thomas Merton, a monk and writer, speaks of the work monks do in the kitchen or fields that then allows them to study, write or pray more effectively. St. Benedict was very well aware of needing a balance in life activities in order to develop our true selves. Most of us are not monks and are engaged in many roles and activities, but having a balance of rushing with slowness, noise and quiet, and light and dark is critical to our well-being as humans. When we believe that everything must be entertaining, be a big deal, or be exciting, we cannot appreciate the balance we need to be our human selves. We lose our creative intuiting for whatever activity in which we engage.

Clarissa Pinkola Estes, PhD, author and Jungian analyst speaks to the cycles of creativity in *The Creative Fire*. One of the aspects of creative living is the dormant period. She suggests that instead of thinking of this state as one of non-productivity, we need to regard this time as one of incubation. During this time mundane activities provide solace and rest for the creative spirit. They relax the overactive mind allowing ideas time to come to maturity. Creative ideas are often not conceived and immediately brought to production. Usually ideas must steep like good brewed tea, or rest like bread dough before shaping. Without allowing this time, the creative idea does not reach its full potential. It lacks the verve and sparkle it could have had if it was allowed to mature appropriately. Without time it struggles to stay alive. Without time, it can become forced, strained and difficult.

So, do something mundane, give yourself a chance to be the human being you can be... relaxed, intentional, thoughtful, loving and creative. Try it for a month – iron, peel carrots, grow a flower, dig in the dirt, chop firewood, listen to yourself – breathe.

I am married to a professional engineer. I worked for 40 years as an occupational therapist and also have written one memoir which was self-published, and a book on Shelton, WA for Arcadia Publishing which is currently in print. I have written and published articles and essays in several anthologies. I am a member of the Pacific Northwest Writers Association, Society of Children's Book Writers and Illustrators, National League of American Pen Women and Nebraska Writer's Guild. I have one son who lives with his family in Washington State.

JOANNE RUSSO INSULL

HELP IN THE TIME OF CORONAVIRUS

I was taught to be a helper, and now at the age of 77, it is deeply ingrained in me. I learned from the Sisters who taught my contemporaries and me and demonstrated by their own lives that we should always be ready to serve, that we should be helpers. We were taught to reach out to others when needed, bringing in food for the poor, visiting nursing homes, reading to children, and we were taught not just to respond to a need, but to be constantly on the lookout for ways we could help others. This is the way I have tried to live my life.

My husband came from a similar background, so we both had similar value systems. We made career choices in line with those values; I chose teaching, he chose psychology. Over the years we became more involved with issues affecting children and adults with disabilities, poverty, health care and literacy. We minister in our parish and in our community. We raised three children who are, I am proud to say, helpers also.

We are what some might describe as 'involved' people, 'responsible' people; caregivers by training and nature, he and I, and we have tried to provide help where needed. It is something we love to do and over our lifetime together we have taken on many causes and advocated for many people. Despite being in our late seventies, we have decent energy levels and can do this. I still work part-time teaching exercise in a local Senior Center.

Then along came COVID-19. The Senior Center was closed, Mass became optional, then moved to a streaming version. We could even eat meat on Fridays in Lent. We had planned a St. Patrick's Day celebration complete with bagpiper and a presentation on Ireland for our parish school, but the school was closed on March 15. Our upcoming activities vanished in the span of 24 hours and our lives became extremely restricted. Our age and vulnerability to the virus required restriction even more than younger people. The things we did as helpers soon morphed into consultations over Zoom.

I had been to the supermarket a couple of days before, so our pantry and fridge contained necessary food items. I unloaded the car, carrying several heavy bags into the house by myself. Toilet paper? A giant package, so we're good. Hand sanitizer? We prefer soap. We have small bottles to use if we need that magic elixir, mostly picked up as free promotional materials at health fairs for Seniors. Dog food? Ordered online. Like I said, we're good.

A young mother in our neighborhood with three little ones expressed concern for my husband and me and offered to shop for us if we needed anything from the store. I thanked her and didn't think about her offer because we have everything we need. Besides, she has three young kids. I should be the one shopping for her. As I was walking our dogs, another young neighbor ordered me not to go out to the stores and told me to call her if we needed something. I thanked her and agreed to call if I needed her. But I knew I wouldn't because I didn't need her. Or did I? I had a totally visceral reaction to her offer. And I wondered...had that time finally come when I could no longer be the helper, the person people rely on? No longer the caregiver? The strong one? Am I ready to give up that part of my life, my spirit? Am I ready to give up control of my life and give it over to the younger generation? That's the key word, right there. Control. I certainly do not want to give up control, to become dependent on others. I'm not sure I can even think about doing that. Hopefully this pandemic will be over soon, my husband and I will survive, and my sense of self, my autonomy, will return. Or will it?

And now we are almost six months into the pandemic. I am grateful that I live in upstate NY. Our state has been fantastic. New Yorkers have been cooperative and caring for each other. They have been the helpers this time. And I think I can live with that.

After many years of working with children and adults with disabilities, I now work part-time teaching Senior Exercise and have written two children's books. I visit schools to read to the children and volunteer as a member of the School Council for St. Ambrose Academy, an elementary school in Rochester, NY.

FRIENDS & COMMUNITY

KAREN CORRELL

HAVOC AND HOPE

Perhaps nowhere are massive contrasts and contradictions more apparent than here in the United States. We are fiercely independent, yet we yearn for togetherness, enjoying gatherings large and small. We dream of working independently from home in our pajamas, yet we crave the camaraderie of team effort, handshakes, high-fives, and a "bless you" when we sneeze. We're obsessed with technology meant to bring us together, knowing full well that it often serves to isolate us, veiling our true humanity from others.

When the novel coronavirus first began making headlines, we mostly regarded it with a collective indifference. We've had our share of maladies, dealt with and largely forgotten. But after a few weeks, it seemed the stories of the insidious spread of the virus had hijacked our news outlets, causing our indifference to turn to annoyance. As coverage became increasingly ubiquitous, lots of folks did their best to ignore it like any other pesky fact of life, such as climate change or seasonal allergies or government corruption or taxes. Soon annoyance became peppered with an existential fear previously unfamiliar to us. We had no idea how to deal. So some people stopped listening to the news completely, and life more or less continued on as normal. Until it didn't.

The day we were sent home from the office to begin quarantine, an ominous cloud hung in the air. Because here in the northeast, nothing stops our work. Snow could pile up for days, but we're armed with our SUVs and trucks with four-wheel drive. The electricity could go out after a windstorm, but we have our generators to handle that. And on the rare occasion that a colleague or a family member passes away, we attend the memorial service, then return to our posts and continue grinding. That's what we do. So when we received the email from our company president sending us home for two weeks, we could no longer ignore the magnitude of COVID-19. I remember watching my colleagues' eyes fill with uncertainty as the grim realization dropped into the pit of my stomach.

Two weeks turned into two months; a brevity attained only because our industry is considered essential; otherwise it would have been far longer. The first few days after being sent home, many of us were consumed with setting up home offices, installing software, and taking work life online. For some this was a long-awaited opportunity to live the fabled 'work in pajamas' lifestyle from home. But what many of us discovered was that as convenient as it was to ditch the commute, we now had a void where the in-person contact had once been. Gone were the smiles, the greetings, the ever-constant presence of others. Working from home was at once liberating and isolating.

In our communities, our fellow humans had morphed into feared instruments of death. No longer could we hug our family members from other households, attend parties, dine at restaurants or shop for anything but food or tools. No sporting events, no movies, no karaoke. As a result, we discovered very quickly that we are ill-suited as social creatures to adapt to this new shape of reality.

My first trip to a store since social distancing guidelines came into effect was a rude awakening into a strange new world. Masks required to enter, hand sanitizing stations in the foyer, one-way arrows in the aisles, and floor markings six feet apart all felt uncomfortably strange. Suddenly, we worry about exchanging money. Touching a surface.

Breathing the air. And we are forced to remind ourselves that if we have money to exchange at all, we are among the fortunate. And if we are still breathing, we are blessed.

The mind-bending stress of isolation has brought out both the best and the worst in people. Opportunists embraced a 'greed is good' perversion of capitalism and engaged in price-gouging that rendered basic supplies completely unattainable by the lower and middle classes. At the same time, we saw people produce masks and sanitizer at home and distribute them for free, or sell them online at cost. Millions lost jobs, while millions more learned genuine gratitude for the work they had not lost. Thousands lost lives, and thousands of lives were saved. While an entitled few unwilling to wear masks took to the streets to protest mandates, millions of others flexibly adapted, determined to do right by others.

Huge swaths of the country are back at 'non-essential' jobs again. We're growing accustomed to wearing masks. We know how to navigate a grocery store. There is talk of a vaccine. In spite of lingering pockets of havoc, people have hope. I like to think that we are slowly emerging from this dark era with a renewed sense of appreciation for all that we had taken for granted, such as human contact, and the ways in which we gather together. We have seen how much we need each other. We have to care about each other because our very survival depends on it. And we need the faraway folks in other countries just as much as our nearby neighbors. With the prevalence of travel and trade, our interdependence is inextricably linked to our quality of life, from the variety of products we enjoy, to the human pool of knowledge, to the diversity of culture that adds strength, depth, and spice to the human experience.

We need a healthy Earth for our global community to call home. How precious were the clear skies when traffic disappeared from the streets! As humanity finds itself in this place of transition and growth, we are bestowed with the perfect opportunity to effect more sweeping change. We must now protect our home in order to protect each other. A small buzz can be heard out there in the ether, but it's gaining volume and scope. Our young people are hearing it, amplifying it, and God willing, the healing of our planet and its people is finally beginning.

Outside of my numbers-based, rational office job, I have interests ranging from metaphysics to human psychology to technology to the environment. I am filled with irrational hope and positive thinking, and wish only for it to be contagious.

John Munn

~

What We Focus on Expands

At this time of extremely serious concern, it is crucial for our collective wellbeing and mental health that we control our thoughts and not allow fear to run rampant within us. Nothing will undermine us personally and the communities we live in faster than mass fear.

Calmness in a time of crises is a priceless commodity at these challenging times.

Be a good neighbor, follow CDC guidelines, be kind, be considerate, treat others with utmost respect, follow social distancing but reach out with your heart.

Live life.

Abundance of care and caution, absolutely! Fear and panic, please no!

The Universe loves everything in balance, the Universe is balance!

So I ask, can you let that balance start with you individually? Take a moment every morning to look within, to quietly reflect. Do I have myself in balance? Am I grounded? Am doing my part to follow the CDC guidelines? Am I being a good neighbor? Am I calm? Am I being a good citizen? Are my thoughts peaceful?

Make this period in which we are being asked to stay at home and isolate ourselves into a Sacred gift to yourself. I believe the Universe is offering us a window, to look within, to reflect and contemplate where might I be out of balance with the world around me? What is going on in me that might be contributing to this worldly chaos? To look and feel where I might need to be healed or experience more inner peace?

I believe we are being offered an opportunity. An opportunity to reboot, to reset how we act towards others, how we behave in the world and how we treat Mother Earth, ourselves and each other. Mother Nature has again shown us the enormity of her power, despite man's best efforts, within a few short weeks the entire world has ground to an almost complete halt.

If you are affected directly by this virus, my thoughts, my prayers and my love are yours. I pray for your speedy recovery. If you are caring for patients with the virus, I love and honor you and I am in awe of your courage, you have the gratitude of us all.

Inner peace will lead to worldly wellbeing. Your inner landscape affects the world you see. Let your thoughts be of healing, wellbeing and peace and the sooner we will see these conditions in the world around us.

We are all in this together. Care for each other. Be there for someone.

I am here for you.

After a long career in the corporate world I am currently training to get certified as a Holistic Spiritual Counselor and I am also working on my first book, a memoir. I contribute everywhere I can, to raising the consciousness of the planet and I am a keen philanthropist.

MISS ME BUT LET ME GO

Standing before the mirror, all clad in black, I sigh. "Do you really think it's necessary to wear the mask?" I ask holding the white surgical mask up to my face. My partner shrugs fixing his tie. I wish I could say that it's a day like any other...but it's not. Today is your funeral.

It's as if the world had stopped in time the moment you took your last breath. As if everyone went into mourning beside us. And rightfully so! You're a celebration of life. You would've laughed at the COVID Pandemic. Not because it's funny, but because it wouldn't intimidate you. Well, that and you would've loved mocking us smokers when the South African tobacco ban finally kicks in.

I know you'd be curious about what's happening in the empty streets of Cape Town, so this is a collection of encounters bathed in your strength, positivity and love for people.

Ordering groceries online was no different from ordering takeout and I quickly fell into the rhythm. After two weeks, however, the effects of COVID had become so overwhelming. People were losing their jobs, children were kept out of school and although I was largely unaffected physically, my emotional health was starting to dip. "How are you?" I ask earnestly as I take the plastic bags from my delivery boy. I could see he was tired, but he smiled and said he was okay. Normally I'd thank the man and retreat to the safety of my apartment, but this time I didn't. We were both wearing masks and keeping our distance, but I never felt so close to a stranger before. We spoke for a while about his family, about work. I asked him if he was scared. He said no. His God was with him.

The COVID pandemic has made me more generous than I could ever dream of being. And not just me. The other day a homeless trumpet player came strolling through the neighbourhood. I stood outside listening. Not long after I noticed little faces begin to pop out of every window, lured by his joyful melody. When the player came into sight, I called to him and gave him shoes. Another man shouted from the top of a high-rise, "wait there, I'll be right down!" and then another and another came rushing to drop loaves of bread, teddies and what have you down balconies and fire escapes.

It was beautiful.

It's funny how I never spoke to my neighbours before this pandemic. I mean, I knew about them and the occasional "hey how are you's" were customary. But I never spoke to them. I never really cared for them. The other day my upstairs neighbour came walking by on her way to the trash depot and she asked if we were moving, which we are. She offered us some boxes and we struck up a conversation. Within minutes she said, "I feel so dizzy," and she slipped down to the floor. My partner and I jumped over our ledge to pick her up and found out that she was pregnant. We never knew. We stayed right below her for nearly two years and we had no idea. She is okay by the way. We walked her back upstairs. And even though I still don't know her name, I care about her now. Weird isn't it?

--

"I'm glad I decided not to wear makeup today," I think, crying as I rise at the end of the funeral service. You slide by in your coffin and it hurts to look. I wish you didn't have to die. But your suffering is over now and I guess you're in a better place.

I wish the COVID Pandemic didn't happen. But strangely I feel like we're in a better place now too. I look down at the memorial card, or funeral order of service and read the line at the back "Miss me, but let me go."

Never has a phrase been more fitting, I think as your funeral ends and the COVID-19 global isolation begins.

Just a girl who writes.

GLORIA DIKEOGU

DANCE

A celebration of life during COVID

Come
Dance with me
Day in
And day out.
Celebrate —
Celebrate with me
That life is worth living
Death is worth dying
But not now —
Not right now.
For right now —
Creativity is all there is.

This first poem was written as I went through day after day of online writing workshops and COVID had prevented our class from travelling to Spain.

REDEFINING MYSELF

I need to find myself
The real me
Hiding beneath the skin
In the depths of soul ----
A self
emerging

Renewed
Reshaped
Redefined

Morphing

GROWING

A sharper image of self
Where
Self and Soul collide.

SILENT STRANGERS

Silence--
The nightly ritual
When pain and suffering knows no bounds.

An endless rhythm of self-talk
Listening to your own voice
As its heightened timber breaks
Across the loud interjections
of the TV anchor.

We are strangers,
    You and I—
Stuck in the constant daily struggle
Yet
Not willing to part
Even when the distance is all we have.

FROM NOWHERE—TO HOPE

Big dreams
    Will take you nowhere

Unless you
> Shoulder the wheel
>> Face your shortcomings head on
> Learn to sacrifice
>> Wrestle with difficulty
> Bank on complexity

Grapple with humility
> Embrace your suffering
>> Consider alternatives

----And in fostering hope
>> Challenge the Fates.

My name is Gloria Dikeogu and I live in Lawrence, Kansas. I am a librarian, college professor, poet and writer. I am currently a student in the Pan-European MFA Program at Cedar Crest College, PA. My previous publications are: a work of poetry, Cape Town Station: a poetic journey *(Short on Time Books) and a children's picture book* Bread! Bread! Bread! *(Rowe Publishing)*

MADHUKANTA SEN

SINCE THE PANDEMIC STRUCK

18th of March, 2020, was our son's birthday. We had made plans to go to Boston and spend a few days with him and his girlfriend there. Our hotel was booked. Right around that time, the coronavirus struck and we had to cancel our trip.

We moved into a townhouse of our own in 2017. We prefer a house which is not totally independent because we have to travel to India every year and it is safer if we have attached neighbors. This year, we are planning to live our winter in the US because travel to India is precarious.

Our son spends his summers with us, here in New Jersey but this year he is spending it in Boston in his own apartment with his girlfriend because she, too, has not travelled to stay with her parents in Jersey.

I was volunteering with the Guggenheim Museum as an Assistant Teaching Artist, commuting to PS38 in Manhattan once every week. That got halted suddenly as the pandemic struck and the academic year got curtailed.

My husband is a professor and his academic year got curtailed as well. He has been teaching online since March.

But the pandemic could not put a stop to other evils. It could not stop George Floyd from getting murdered. And then, the people poured onto the streets. With a unified voice crying "Black Lives Matter," which was the strongest voice ever. A voice so strong that it forced every institution in the country and all over the world to reassess and revamp themselves.

It has been the horrific time of a raging pandemic but it has also been the time of crying out together; crying out in pain as the wounds of injustice were inflicted upon the human souls! Crying out because of the hopelessness of the times!

My life personally, so far, during the pandemic, has been artistically fruitful. I wrote a lot, painted and also recorded a song. All this happened in spite of the downturns which have become a regular part of my life now. I was trolled, was mentally punished for being honest and outspoken, and for expressing my heartfelt desires. As usual.

My husband, Kaustav and I cooked up a variety of delicious dishes during this time. We had sumptuous dinners almost every night!

My health got better from bad and I was able to remain increasingly active.

Now, after five long months, things are gradually beginning to resemble normalcy in our household.

Two of my neighbors and I, started a book club and we met for the first time in our garage in a socially distant manner. Our housekeeper came and spruced up our home after five months. We spent the time when she was here, going out and roaming a park close by. My artist friend dropped by and we discussed a collaborative project for the USPS. I accompanied Kaustav to a close by Pier 1 Imports one day and experienced actual shopping after all these months!

Should we say we can, now, "Hope for the Best"?

The pandemic has shown us, by restricting us humans, that the planet is in much better shape when we do not impose upon it our zillion acts prompted by greed. By our efforts directed towards squeezing out more and more of its last resources. For our own benefit. We bring upon the other species inhabiting this planet of ours, innumerable injustices.

We must curb ourselves. We must care about all our cohabitants, beginning from other human beings who are not privileged. If we do so, only then will God be sated and will not punish us.

Madhukanta Sen is an Indian artist based in Clifton, New Jersey. Her practice is concentrated in painting, poetry and vocal music. She is poised to exhibit her work with RAW Artists in New York City and other cities in the United States. Sen is an Assistant Teaching Artist with the Guggenheim Museum's Learning Through Art program. Her poetry has been published in The Telegraph, The Poetry Guild, *and* Hello Poetry. *Madhukanta Sen holds a Master's degree in Fine Arts from Montclair State University and a Master's degree in Comparative Literature from Jadavpur University, India.*

SUSYN REEVE

LIGHT IN THE TUNNEL OF UNCERTAINTY

As 2020 approached, I rented my nieces' condo in Wilmington, North Carolina for the winter. I had a plan. I was certain.

Once unpacked and settled in the condo I created a roadmap for the new business I committed to launching, *Lead with Love: Creating Your Life from the Inside Out.* Armed with this roadmap, I stepped fully into 2020 with certainty. I had a plan.

Then COVID-19 made a grand entrance.

My niece, during the winter, usually spent three to five days a month at the condo. Now, in the midst of COVID-19, she needed to be there full-time for her home healthcare business. *Sharing the condo could be fun,* I thought. I like my niece! Then the schools in North Carolina closed, and her husband began working from home. Plans changed. Now my niece, her family – two teenagers, one husband, and one dog would all be living in their 2-bedroom condo, three hours from their house.

Humm, time to make a new plan. Where to live? Then I had an idea, I'll ask friends, Lynn & Bob, on Hilton Head Island, SC if it's a good time to visit. How long could COVID really last? Lynn's response was immediate, "Sure, come on down." Again, I had a plan.

Other than being in another state, with special friends, life wasn't much different than I expected. Beautiful weather, frequent walks, afternoons on the empty beach, delicious dinners, and plenty of time to focus on getting my *Lead with Love courses*, workshops, and coaching online.

Then in April, friends mothers' - one 92, another 102 - died within a week of being diagnosed with COVID; and my beloved hometown, New York City, was the epicenter of an astounding daily death count, with bodies stored in refrigerated trucks, and a field hospital set up in Central Park. Clearly a quick end to COVID-19 was not in sight. It was time to find light in this tunnel of uncertainty.

I felt the call of the northeast.

I had thought I'd stay on Hilton Head for a week, maybe ten days. But, it was two months before I was on the road again, with a full gas tank, mask, gloves, hand sanitizer, and food. First to Wilmington, to pack and then to Hampton Bays, NY, stopping in Manhattan for two nights. I had a plan.

May 9th. After driving 10 hours I arrived in NYC, with alternate-side of the street parking suspended and the streets practically traffic-free. Even in the midst of a global pandemic, there are moments when gratitude abounds. This was one of those times. I'd arrived safely in Manhattan and parked easily around the corner from where I was staying!

May 10th. I woke excited to be in my hometown for another day. At 6:50pm, accessorized with a mask and gloves, I took the elevator downstairs and gathered with other masked people to cheer and celebrate Lenox Hill Hospital frontliners.

I noticed a car parked catty-corner on the northwest corner of East 77th St. There were two or three Orthodox Jewish men (I'm Jewish, I recognized their garb) setting up a microphone and amplifier. At exactly 7pm standing atop the car hood, one of the men began singing. First *The Star Spangled Banner*, with rousing cheers when the words *Land of the Free* and *Home of the Brave* were sung. Amidst this celebration of appreciation, a police car stopped, joining the cheering and honking as the second song, *You Raise Me Up,* with lyrics honoring the health care workers, filled the street.

I was thrilled to be part of this gathering in the safety of my hometown neighborhood. The cheering and honking were the perfect accompaniment to the singing. Every cell of my body was bathed in Love and appreciation. Tho' faces were masked, smiles were in the air. The singing ended. The police car turned the corner, to cheers and applause, and drove away.

Moments later a young black man walked by, talking to no one in particular. His words captured my attention: *Yeah, you're applauding here. This isn't what goes on in my neighborhood. Here's someone standing on the hood of a car giving a concert, the police participate and simply drive away. Come to my neighborhood, it's not like this. Someone could get killed in my neighborhood for singing atop a car hood. Yeah, just keep on applauding and cheering.*

My eyes followed him as he continued walking toward Park Avenue. I felt as though I'd been stabbed in my heart. I thought of Ahmaud Arbery, murdered while jogging. A modern day lynching. I was in an affluent very white neighborhood. I'm white and privileged. This young black man reminded me that the virus of racism, Kills.

The vaccine for Hate is needed. We know what the remedy is. It's Love in Action.

As I entered the apartment, the pain in my heart took hold of my body. I wondered, *What is the Love in Action for me to take? How do I lead with Love?*

On May 25, 2020 George Floyd was murdered and the world - particularly much of the white world woke up. I am grateful for this wake-up. Not like the celebratory cheering on the evening of May 10th; rather to have been woken up to my internalized racism; woken up to my ignorance of Black History - which *is* American History.

I'm inspired and grateful to step-by-step, sometimes stumbling, take an active role in nourishing the promise of the United States of America to form a more perfect Union of Life, Liberty, and the Pursuit of Happiness for *All* People.

As COVID-19 continues to spike in California, Texas, Arizona, and Florida, I'm seeing and feeling light in the tunnel, as I deepen and expand my commitment to Lead with Love, which has been my plan, my certainty, since 2020 began!

My north star is a question I wrote in my journal when I was 14-years old: What would the world be like if everyone loved themselves? *I am the creator of* Lead with Love Coaching and the author of Heart Healing: The Power of Forgiveness to Heal a Broken Heart, The WholeHearted Life, and The Inspired Life.

ROGER NASON

THE RIDE

2020. What a year. For many it will be remembered as nothing but bad. For me, though, I will always remember it for the roller coaster ride it was. It was a bad year, yet it was a great year. Most certainly a year I will never forget.

It started off on a high note. My girlfriend and I rang in the New Year in the Canary Islands. We had a blast. Of course, at this point neither one of us had heard about the coronavirus. We enjoyed the island life staying at a 5-star hotel and really just living it up.

Once we arrived home, we settled back into our normal lives. However, about two weeks later, we both got sick. Very sick. We went to the walk-in clinic and they tested us for the flu. They informed us that the tests were positive. We had the flu, even though we both had gotten flu shots.

We got our prescriptions and we went home. Later that night my fever continued to spike. My girlfriend brought me to the emergency room and they admitted me overnight due to my blood oxygen levels being so low. Turned out that I had pneumonia too.

While lying in the hospital bed I started hearing about this virus in China, but at that time it seemed no different than SARS or the Bird Flu. Those had not turned out to be anything big, at least not so much in the U.S.

I went home and after a week or so the symptoms started to subside. All was well.

A month later towards the end of February, I got sick again. I went to the hospital and sure enough I had pneumonia again, this time on the other lung. This was accompanied by the worst body aches I think I ever had. Again, it subsided in about a week.

As an aside, my girlfriend is convinced that we had COVID-19. The circumstances and timing certainly make that a possibility, but we will likely never know for sure.

Since I was sick though, I started to work from home so I didn't infect anyone at the office, especially if it was the coronavirus. About two weeks later my company announced that everyone should work from home due to the pandemic.

March was a boring month. Stuck at home with no place to go and the weather was not cooperating either. We were both starting to go a bit stir crazy. I spent most of the month worrying about my girlfriend, who is a nurse. She was working at elderly care facility and COVID-19 was spreading through many of these facilities in the area. One more thing to worry about.

Enter April. Did I mention that I have a son in the US Navy? Well, he is stationed in South Korea, and was supposed to be coming home this month after completing his two-year duty assignment there. Thanks to the world-wide pandemic, this did not happen.

What a year right? It couldn't get any worse, right? Wrong. In mid-April, I got my lay-off notice. My employer of the past 13 years was restructuring and my job was being eliminated. Little did I know, this was the beginning of the high point of the year so far.

I had been hinting to my girlfriend for the past few months that we should get married, but we never pushed it. My girlfriend took the bull by the horns and she finally said, "Let's get married". Four days later I got down on one knee and proposed, with a beautiful ring that I ordered through a local jeweler - since we were on a stay-at-home order and all the brick and mortar stores were closed. Obviously, she said yes!

About a week later a former coworker reached out to me about the layoffs my company just had. I mentioned to her that I was a bit nervous, as it was not a good time to be laid-off in the midst of the COVID-19 crisis. Surprisingly, her response to me was, "We are hiring."

By the end of the day she had my resume. The following week the company reached out to me. Within two weeks I had been offered a job with a pay raise.

Things were certainly looking up. I had a job and would be starting on June 1. We had a wedding date for August 1. The planning and doing was well underway.

About this time, I got confirmation from my son in the Navy that he would be coming home a few days before the wedding. Things were falling into place. This was starting to look like a great year for us.

In June, my girlfriend also lost her job. You may think that is another strike against 2020. However, this is what I wanted and she needed. The job was stressing her out, both of us really. In addition, we had much to do with our wedding less than two months away. The job loss was another blessing in disguise. She could now take some time off before the wedding, and for the honeymoon too. After the honeymoon she will look for the right job. The job that makes her happy. My job pays enough to cover us until she finds her 'happy place' job.

So here we are, less than a month until our wedding. Everything is falling into place. We will be honeymooning in a cottage on a lake, until it is safe to travel again. Then I will take her to the Caribbean for a real honeymoon.

In short, while many suffered and found the year to be filled with loneliness and pain, we managed to find our way to happiness, and the entire year has turned into an incredible year that neither one of us will ever forget. 2020 is the year I married my soulmate and my best friend. 2020 is the beginning of our happily ever after.

I am the father of two adult boys. I am in love with the woman of my dreams. We live in southeastern New Hampshire. I am also an aspiring author. I have one novel with an editor at this time.

ANN HALL

THE HISTORY LESSON

Alice Herman died 51 years and five days before I was born. By all accounts, my father's Aunt Alice was a healthy 14-year-old one day, and was gone the next, one of 675,000 American victims of the Influenza Epidemic of 1918. Her younger sisters didn't get sick. My great-grandmother Grace did, but she recovered quickly. Alice was just an unwilling participant of a bizarre game of viral Russian Roulette.

We had a few pictures of Alice in our house. I didn't look like anyone else in the family as a child, but I could have been Alice's twin. When I was little, this made me so sad, this loss of chance. I got it in my head that once I reached 14, it was my responsibility to enjoy life for both of us. I grew out of this admittedly strange promise to a long-gone girl, and honestly gave very little thought to her over the years. She became just another family story, a comment made when we looked at old photos. Now I am an adult, a mother and a wife. I have two degrees and have traveled a good part of the world. But this is my first pandemic. So now it's Alice's turn to help me.

I love history and I love to dig down into a topic. My reaction to the current pandemic is to try to understand – to learn what people were saying and thinking and feeling during previous pandemics to give me a clue on how this is going to go. Alice and her family left nothing in writing on the subject, or if they did, it's long gone. My grandmother died before I was born and the youngest of the Herman girls died 30 years ago. But there are a plethora of interviews recorded in the 1980s and 1990s of people who lived through that time, who nursed family members and buried them too. There was no cure and there was no effective treatment. The only thing health officials could do was remind people to physically distance, practice good hygiene and wear a mask. Sound familiar?

I have read the newspaper stories and historians' work. I have read the grim statistics. It's remarkable. The reactions were the same. The suspicion and the fear were the same. The hoax rumors spread faster than the flu. Americans turning on each other and away from their neighbors and friends had to be depressing and frustrating in 1918. I know this because it certainly is causing Alice's great-niece anxiety now. I am trying to take comfort from fact that while the country was tearing itself apart in 1918, it survived. Alice's sisters went on to school, marriage and motherhood. People enjoyed life again and we will too.

I am a proud mother of two wonderful boys, a voracious reader and a firm believer that education can come in many forms.

Alice Herman

ROSANNE GROSS

COVID DREAMIN'

It was the worst of times. It was the best of times. The Spring of 2020.

I found true love in the last few years, with great surprise, coming late in life. My fella is Canadian and I am American. Neither of us was perfectly happy in our own countries, but we knew we were happy with each other.

We were very lucky to get to spring of 2020. Very lucky despite – or indeed, because of – cancer treatments and job difficulties to get to have a respite from the world in the form of a cruise. It would be a fantasy to live for ten days, the longest vacation I had ever taken, a celebration of a new lease on life. We heard rumblings of the virus, many chose not to go on the trip, but we packed Lysol spray and wipes and traveled anyway.

The trip was nothing short of amazing, rock-and-roll music and a Grand Cayman island sparkling lagoon. Simply put, magical!

When we came back down to earth and arrived back in Port Everglades, there was a ship that the Uber driver pointed out that could not disembark. The virus was now in Florida. It begins.

After arriving home, there were virus cases reported by the local port workers. We strained our minds to recall if we were near anyone coughing, thought hard about what we had touched. My Canadian friend took his temperature regularly. I prayed.

Then the world seemed to explode. Locked down businesses, counties, states. It put me in a daze, completely unbelievable. The toilet paper search.

My partner and I had been seeing each other every three or four weeks or so for two years and these visits had become the highlight of our lives. I listened carefully to talk of closing the United States border with Canada. Borders were closed to all other international travelers and Canadians were advised to return home from abroad immediately or potentially be shut out in the future, but travel between the US and Canada remained open. Then an outcry in the Canadian press as cases ramped up in New York. They did not want the poorly managed American virus cases to leach into Canada. The border would be locked down completely.

That morning after listening to the news, I paced. I anguished. If the borders were closed when could I see my love again? The soap opera in my head warned we could each die alone without ever having said goodbye. A million questions went through my mind, I was terrified to go, terrified to stay.

I called the border offices on March 18th; they said the border had been closed at noon to all nonessential travel. I asked what exactly is 'essential'. They replied that had not been clarified as yet so it was up to the border patrol officer at the gate to determine that decision. Ah, a window.

In a heartbeat I threw everything I might need into my tiny red Mazda3 and hit the road.

I got to the border crossing at 1am. It was deserted but for one agent. With two large dogs sleeping in the back seat and a pet carrier in the front passenger seat with my Sun Conure, Summer, holding my fingers tightly through the grate, we met our fate. Would Canada let us in?

The border guard took a look at my credentials, but did a triple take at the bird next to me. "Do you have papers for that bird?" he asked. After my explanation he shrugged, handed me a COVID-19 information sheet and waved me through. After all that worry, I couldn't believe it, I was in!

After a couple more hours of driving, I stopped for a break. In the parking lot there were people with full gas masks on, and many campers parked with those obviously fleeing the cities. It seemed like an apocalypse movie in the middle of the night.

Walking the dogs, watching classic movies and playing endless games were a pure gift for me. If you could avoid listening to the news for a moment, and if you could pay today's bills and not think about tomorrow's, it felt like more vacation time. Walking miles and miles across Montreal in the snow and rain with no others on the street was like a private showing of the beautiful old city. We discovered a priceless treasure of sites that would never be seen so peacefully under normal circumstances.

My partner began to work seven days a week, sometimes 14-hour days in an attempt to save his restaurant from failure. The Canadian government's subsidies and loans are helpful, but don't really make a dent in recovering the financial losses that small-to-medium businesses are having to sustain. One after the other began to close permanently in his neighborhood.

I expected borders between the countries to open in late June and so reluctantly arranged to return to Chicago. As much as I hated but loved this COVID-cation I heard the insistent voice of reality at home in a pile of unopened bills and an untended yard.

Before I left Canada, I overheard my partner explaining to someone, "She came up from the States and has been here for three months, it's been glorious!" And indeed, it has.

Borders have remained closed now going on six months. Even adult children seeking to be with their dying parents have been denied Canadian entry, along with couples that cannot prove documented common law status.

My friends say life is short, I continue to dream.

We are in a pandemic, the economy is horrible, many tragedies have occurred and precious lives have been lost. But it could always be worse, we could be in England in World War II with bombs crashing into our homes. We could be in a civil war with soldiers marching through our yards.

We will prevail. We have been in worse times. We will get through this together. Dream big.

Summer 2020.

I have worked in the accounting field my whole life but am also a Reiki Master Teacher, Bach Flower Essence practitioner, house renovator and am now dabbling with words.

REGINA MARIE WOODWARD

#LOVEINTHETIMEOFCORONA

My husband and I had been separated for two years when he saw my profile on Tinder. Living in separate countries, I had come to visit him on a short travel layover.

I hadn't thought to turn off the dating app, so when I landed in a new country, I was automatically shuffled to the top of the stack of fresh available women, in a Muslim country, where the women on dating apps are few and the men are many.

I had landed in the morning and arrived at the house right before he went off to work. That evening I heard his keys jingle in the lock. It had been nearly a year since we had last been around each other.

He opened the door, "I saw your profile on Tinder today."

I grimaced. "Which way did you swipe?" I asked.

My husband and I had been separated for three years when we travelled back home together from overseas to visit our families for the summer. I travelled from the country I lived in to meet him for our international flight. We held hands and ordered more drinks as we flew over the Pacific.

Over the summer, we told our friends and family members, one by one, that we were separated. My husband cried when we went through our storage in my mom's attic, dividing our things.

I told a few friends the Tinder story over drinks, which always ended, "He is the best thing I've found on Tinder."

My husband and I have been separated for nearly four years when I planned a weekend layover to visit him on my way to India and Nepal. A week before I am to leave, India shuts its borders to travel, then a few days before, Malaysia announces its borders will close before I'm due to arrive.

Immediately, I know, there's only one place I want to be in the grand uncertainty of a pandemic. I change my ticket and leave the next morning to travel. A Muppets song plays in my head on a loop, "There's not a word yet, for old friends who've just met."

I spend twelve weeks with my husband in his apartment under an extreme Movement Control Order and lockdown. We talk. We cook. We trigger each other. We watch movies. We play chess. We talk more. We laugh. We cook again. We trigger each other's triggers, but it's not like before.

There are no drinks this time. There is no escaping one another. There's only growth and getting to know who this new person is in front of each of us. The triggers become this funny sort of view, as if I can see through a mirror for a new perspective. Being around each other becomes as easy as breathing.

He's still the best thing I've found on Tinder.

Regina is originally from the green and lush West Coast forests of the USA. True to her lineage of American pioneers, she has spent the past decades as an explorer, living abroad.

LORETTA DEL GRECO

71 IN SICILY!

With my milestone 70th birthday approaching, my family and I were planning on celebrating it together in Sicily, the home of our maternal grandparents. We were in the fun, exploratory phase of what to do once we got there – Greek ruins, volcanoes, wine and lots of food. Before we could book the first flight or lodging – coronavirus hit and altered not only these plans but many others. Now, of course I understand that many of us have it so much worse with illness and job loss. Luckily, we have been spared that. This is just the tale of one woman's quest for serenity and connection during this difficult time.

Sicily would have to wait for next year – we would celebrate it BIG in 2021! But how to get through these next months? My grown children lived out of the area, as did my brother's family. We decided as a family to do what we could to stay safe which meant no visits in person. Lucky for me, I have a dog and a boyfriend (ridiculous word at our ages) who lives nearby. My kids were working remotely and I am retired, so there was no added job worry stress. We were in pretty good shape. I reminded myself how strong I was, left alone when my kids were two and four, and raising two great human beings on my own on a schoolteacher's salary. I lived in Florida and the beach was five minutes away! We got this!

Being a creature of habit, my first attempt was to build in some structure to days that could feel endless. Coffee and

THE CORONA SILVER LININGS ANTHOLOGY

newspaper – check! Walk dog – check! Straighten house – check! Exercise – check! Shower and get ready for the day – check! Great, that could take me to eleven or noon, the question was; then what? Unable to do many usual activities (gym, restaurants, browsing thrift stores, volunteering at the food bank), I had to rethink it all.

It seemed like my creative juices were flowing. The internet has an abundance of Bob Ross videos which inspired me to try my hand at painting. I always have loved writing and have written many things for the family – so I continued that by creating some pandemic fairy tales (illustrated with my newfound artistic skills) for the little ones of the family. Knitting reemerged, an activity I hadn't done since high school. So far, one scarf in the Christmas gift drawer. My freezer became loaded with homemade cookies and quick breads – oh yes, lots of meatballs too. I had time to delve more deeply into family ancestry. I signed up for Zoom piano lessons and improved my Italian skills online as well. My garden thrived and supplied us with tomatoes, basil, scallions and mint. Of course, tons of books were read and more TV was watched than I care to admit. Eventually, I joined a monthly social distance book club that met on the beach, and a political support group that met online. Staying occupied was becoming more possible.

The biggest hurdle was connection – with family, friends and loved ones. The phone was a lifeline, and I wrote more letters than ever – real letters, not just email. Every Sunday night my entire family would get together via Zoom – it was our happy hour, wine in hand, and after a few weeks we added trivia to our weekly meetings. I sure did miss my kids though, and I know I'm not alone in that! On my 70th birthday (yes, that one, the one we were all supposed to be in Sicily), my son showed up and we social-distanced outside all afternoon and it was wonderful (and safe!). I advised my daughter who lived in another state not to take a chance coming to Florida whose numbers were so bad. But did she

199

have a surprise for me. That night on Zoom it wasn't just our immediate family, she'd contacted extended family and many friends, and I was shocked and a bit overwhelmed to be surrounded by so much unexpected and very much appreciated love. A 70th birthday I'll never forget! I guess my take on all this is that it's been difficult at times, I don't want to sugar coat it, but it's doable if we focus on the things we CAN do rather than the things we CANNOT do.

It's going to be so great when we all get back to our 'new normal', whatever that is. This experience has chiseled away lots of superfluous stuff and reminded us all the importance, the necessity of connection, of love. I feel it and I look forward to celebrating in an even bigger way in 2021 with my family in Sicily! Blessings to all and Ciao!

I loved my 30-plus-year career as an elementary school counselor, and was happily spending my retirement these last few years enjoying travel and family until COVID hit. Now I visit my family on Zoom and am in the process of building a different sort of life –for now –while looking forward to returning to 'normal' one day!

EFRAT MALACHI

THE HUMAN SPIRIT

Managing COVID-19 these past six months has been both grueling and growth-orienting. With the virus taking our global community by storm, we've had to quickly relearn the vernacular of mankind by reuniting on a basic, humane level. This unique situation has enabled me to see through the sophisticated opaque reality we've created in the name of a civil society. Although law and order are essential, we equally cannot live without the intentions and spirit of the laws which are often overshadowed by its text. We're so used to having rules tell us how to go about our days as individuals and as the groups we're categorized into based on our lifestyles. And being the social creatures that we are, connection and affection are necessities that don't always identify clear boundaries. That's why having official standards are a significant part of structured living, but I believe in order for it to be healthy it needs restrictions of its own. Now that I can compare people's attitudes before Corona and during it, societal rules and regulations (usually strict and uncompromising) are what I've found to have gotten lost in translation within everyday life. This has led us to doubt our overarching humanity that subtly highlights everything we do.

With the coronavirus, these rules have been overridden and proven not immune to life's nature. It has shown me that not everything can be solved with a political speech or passed bill. We need more than protocols to sustain our society. Remember that behind every signature and stamp is a real person who breathes the same air and cares. Experts, scholars, and professionals are just as vulnerable as a blade of grass is to the wind. COVID-19 has awakened me to how we all share a common weakness that is also our biggest strength and solution for these times – free will. Our ability to choose gives us authority over the things we do but can too overstep others' freedom to do the same, so we must be cautious. It lets us cross out conventions for the sake of doing the right thing. It demands the black and white be blended, the rules be bent and even broken. This navigating through countless shades of gray is what's most intimidating and challenging yet necessary in times of crisis.

This new-founded reality has created further epiphanies. I've come to internalize deeply that behind every professional is truly a regular person with strong established habits, not a superhero or natural born leader. As an example of this (only a few months ago), while speaking on the phone with my parents' health insurance, it was surprising to hear a soft voice on the other end genuinely ask how we're all doing and wishing us well when the conversation was over. Another similar instance happened while chatting online with Citibank's customer service. Empathetic messages were exchanged between me and the representative who had always felt robotic in the past but now was someone I could recognize. Later when scrolling through the chat history, I was moved to see how it was full of sincere nuanced expressions; it was clear this could only be a human's doing. We're accustomed to thinking of the other side, the professionals in chat rooms or phone conversations, as AI (artificial intelligence) in disguise but they're simply people trained to stick to a script. It was intensely relieving to experience the breaking of barriers and the unveiling of truths behind these norms. Because here and now, people weaved emotions into their messages and did not act like cold characters. In both episodes, it no longer felt like a foreign being helping me with the ins and outs of life but an authentic human journeying with me through it.

A more personal lesson I've learned is that to be a champion you must battle the demons of the present day, not of yesterday nor of tomorrow. When you take things one step at a time, as cliché as it is, you really can walk up any and every flight you face. All it takes is passion and persistence. If along the way you encounter a loose step, don't be afraid to keep charging upwards because you have the support of those steps beneath which you've climbed and the future ones above ready to embrace you. And if you fall, that's nothing to be ashamed of either. It's a process of expanding and enlightening which makes the view at the top worthwhile. Another lesson I've picked up, nothing is ever set in stone although people have the confidence to convince us that it is so. Fashions and trends are constantly evolving, so never be afraid to have an opinion on them because they will waver. The one thing that shouldn't is your beliefs which can always be a trustworthy guide through the ever-changing political/social climates.

Something new I've discovered about myself during this time is that whenever I say, "I'm done, I'm wiped", I'm really maybe 60% done. Although there are moments when life doesn't spare me the 'fair' card, when I just think of going to sleep and waking up again, then I instantly feel relieved. Regarding self-care during Corona, I learned how key it is to our existence and overall happiness. Taking proper care of one's self with sufficient sleep, water, meals, exercise, and recreation is non-negotiable. The lack of this has taught how much of the ordinary and 'same old' we have to be grateful for. There are no deadlines or perfect way to love and nurture one's whole self, as Nike says – just do it. Simply keep yourself working a bit better than you were the day before; nothing has to be too crazy or conventional. Finally, you decide how and where life's magic will reveal itself to you.

Efrat is a graduate of Yeshiva University and a self-published author/ poet. She is a creative storyteller and deep thinker sparking authentic conversations on her social media platforms.

EVERYTHING OLD IS...

I feel for those affected and our first responders. I watch my wife, a teacher, grapple and struggle to find a meaningful way to reach the hundreds of students she so deeply cares for, constantly worried that 'she's not enough'. I finally attempt to clean the garage and sort through the dozens of boxes neglected by the man on a rat wheel, the constant churning of supposed forward motion. I watch the headlines grow more and more unimaginable. I meditate? Say whaaa?

For 30-plus years I taught students. And they...taught ME. They created films, poetry, theatre and performance art. They constructed and deconstructed media, video games, films and technology. But they also taught me the life lessons that I now put in play in the eeriest of circumstances. The guiding questions asked of them then now lead to the practices and principles that guide MY days.

Who created the message? What creative techniques are used to attract my attention? How might someone different than me view this message differently? I'd never heard of the 5 Key Questions That Can Change the World (Center for Media Literacy). Our year-long project-based learning assignment (aptly entitled THE ASSIGNMENT) forced us out of the box in 2006. Our film 'Don't Hate, Communicate' brought us conflict resolution techniques, Media Literacy as Violence Prevention, examining fake news, studying bias, deciphering misinformation and disinformation. The lack of a brick-and-mortar room led to Viola Spolin and Augusto

Boal games played outside in an empty parking lot and eventually, an old brick building in Van Nuys that housed mindfulness, yoga and meditation on a daily basis.

Speaking truth to power brought us to Get Lit and that non-profit then transformed our classroom, school and community. Now I tune in to free classes and workshops via Get Lit to improve my own literacy skills (some taught by former students). Most recently, Inner City Shakespeare partnered BAFTA actors with professionals and novices here at our newly formed HelMel Studios in Los Angeles as they 'pivoted' the production of Romeo and Juliet to Zoom and yes, once again...ART SAVED LIVES.

Does it need to be said? Does it need to be said now? Does it need to be said by me? The 'THINK' methodology is a thing. (Is it thoughtful? Honest? Intelligent? Necessary? Kind?) Does the Light, Bright and Polite strategy that we read about almost a decade ago apply to the social media of the present?

I now find myself employing the communication skills and tricks that were once simply words on a page, dyads and triads in action, now the very foundation of how I navigate through our daily team meetings and business interactions in our Film and TV Projects, newly formed Twainmania Foundation and Technology Companies like SparkRise. Hell, SparkRise was literally based on a school event in 2011 where we staged a 'happening' and raised funds in a new and exciting way...a better, faster, easier way. While I've stepped away from the classroom, that experience drives the desire to find new ways for schools and nonprofits to raise funds, communicate and take the 'pain' out of the process.

We explored the word 'empathy' in myriad fashion while we discussed how the word 'gratitude' would hang on signs in classrooms in the 21st century. We did not know WHY. We just KNEW. I certainly had no idea that I would make it my morning ritual and that it would provide light through the darkness.

Quite frankly, while engaging, all of this was academic until this global pandemic. Now it resonates and dictates daily practice. Now I find myself digging through old curriculum and re-reading lessons and student assignments of the past.

But most importantly, now I am open to staying present, willing to embrace change and employing "acceptance" as a way of practicing LOVE... Letting Others Voluntarily Evolve. It's time to LISTEN and it's time to listen to the many much younger than myself. Student becomes teacher. Mentees become mentors. I think my favorite thing about teaching is, if you turn young people onto cool "s#$%", MAGIC happens. And if you truly put relationships at the forefront of your teaching, the development, cultivation and maintenance of these lifelong relationships leads to collaboration on a cosmic level. The collaboration becomes organic, the process...joyous. Bring it. Class is in session.

I am the Producer of Shakespeare High, Cinema Twain and Co-Founder of Sparkrise. I am an educator, filmmaker, entrepreneur and arts advocate. Over the past 25 years, I have taught courses in film, theatre, media literacy, communications and digital humanities.

Brad Koepenick and his students

SICKNESS, LOSS; HEALING & HEALTH

George Byram

In 1918, the worldwide Spanish Flu pandemic traveled the globe and snuck into the last moments of George Byram's childhood, killing his mother. Fall had brought a heavy and hard reality to the Byram family. George's little sisters had been back at school for a few months when they both caught influenza. Fevers, chills, and heavy coughs slowed the usually giggly girls down, but their mother spent hours rubbing eucalyptus oil on their chests, making them gargle with salt water, and keeping them in cool clean sheets. This routine only lasted a few days before Annie couldn't get out of bed. What had been a slight sickness for the girls, turned dangerous for her. Annie was still recovering from a miscarriage and within three days she could no longer fight the fluid in her lungs. George wanted more time with her, wanted a proper goodbye, wanted her comfort, and more than anything wanted her to stay.

It was hard to not let sadness swallow him up with two little girls in the house who needed to be taken care of, who needed a mother. George knew he and his father had tried their best to let the girls say goodbye. There was no funeral; a strict quarantine was in place. Instead, George and his dad wheeled their mother's coffin to the bay window on the side of the house so everyone could safely see her one last time. No undertaker would dig her grave because she died of the Spanish Flu. George and his dad took their shovels and chiseled away at the frozen November ground, so she would have somewhere to rest. After the sudden and heartbreaking loss, it was George and his father who had to sit down in the family parlor and sort out the necessary logistics for the rest of their lives. Huddled over a cup of coffee in a red brick farmhouse, a teenage boy and a widower let go of the roles they were supposed to play and took on the ones they now had to play. They took a new path to help their family climb out of the devastating sadness of what just happened.

In 1918, mothers had the sole responsibility for raising children and running households. Affection, security, warmth, and food were the main descriptions of her job title and like today, the main emotional components needed to raise stable children who contribute to society in meaningful ways. Taking her out of the delicate balance of a family unit leaves scars and wounds that heal and split open throughout life, so when the Byrams sat in their parlor, fire roaring and tears flowing, they made a decision. Life would be different. A void would have to be filled, and the most unlikely and unusual character would have to spend the rest of his life doing just that. Seventeen-year-old George Byram would let go of his dreams, disregard stereotypes, and put his sorrow and whole soul into raising his little sisters. One hundred and two years later, looking at the past and understanding the scope of George Byram's selfless actions can provide a clear route to give us hope and move us forward.

The 1918 pandemic stole much from the Byrams, but it taught the Byrams to find a new approach. It taught them to take a new path that eventually brought them peace, strengthened their family, and restored their hope. The business of moving forward forced the Byrams to decide what kind of life they wanted to have. Each member of the family was recognized for the gifts they naturally possessed and the whole family used those gifts and abilities to help each other survive and then once again thrive.

George Byram had a special way with his little sisters. He was the most capable one in the family to nurture the girls as closely to the way their mother had. His talents and abilities did not conform to the belief system at that time, but he embraced his new role and shrugged off the old ways of doing things because they were no longer relevant. He quietly put silly notions to rest and spent his days raising his sisters. George and his dad, William, worked the family farm together, but George spent the mornings, afternoons, and evenings with his sisters. He was devoted.

He learned to braid hair and bought them matching ribbons with their school dresses. He packed lunches and made sure they had coats and warm shoes that fit in the winter. He helped them with homework and heard all about the happenings in the classroom and in the schoolyard. George was the one who decided they should take piano lessons and found them a teacher, bought them a piano, and delivered them to their weekly lessons. He must have had a system to get them to practice, because they both learned how to read music and enjoy it. When they were teenagers, he found out that nylons and lipstick were essential and always made sure they had money to buy them. George was affectionate, patient, and kind. He remained a bachelor until he was thirty-six years old and saw both his sisters marry before he did.

My grandpa George probably never gave himself enough credit for what he did as a teenage boy. Did he think about how reassuring his hugs felt to those little girls and how big of a void he filled in their lives? He kept it simple and focused on what he could do. He let go of a role he was supposed to play and lived a new life with the gifts and talents he had. Out of necessity, the 1918 Spanish Flu pandemic turned him into a mother. Pandemics hand down many difficult realities, but a century ago a seventeen-year-old gave us a glimpse of all that is possible when we let go of how we think things should be and make room for them to be better.

Erika Taylor lives in Calgary Canada. She loves sunshine and skiing and enjoys travelling with her family.

Tim Morrison, DMin, ND

~

The Light Continues to Shine and the
Darkness Cannot Overcome It

We, as chaplains, are never permitted to share medical information with families. That is not our arena. With coronavirus, though, our work as chaplains has become more family focused. We telephone patient's families or FaceTime. We identify ourselves as chaplains. We ask, "What can we do for you? More importantly, how are you doing?" And the words flow. We hear the hurts, the worries, the anxieties, the uncertainties and of course the hopes... We hear it all. We do our best to get messages to the medical team when families ask questions. In turn we share the responses. Families understand the pressure doctors and nurses and all medical staff are under. So, we offer ourselves as conduits, short cuts if you will, for exchange of information, to provide encouragement to the medical team as expressed by their patients' families and assurance to the families that there is a way to get a word to the medical team.

And when we engage in those conversations with the medical teams, we take time to ask about them – just give us a one-word answer if that is all time allows...but we have time to listen if you want to talk or even simply pretend to talk so you can have a bit of a quiet moment. More times than not we hear, "Thank you" followed by soft uh, huh, yes, uh huh, nothing more. We know our colleague is making use of the proffered quiet time. Then we hear a firm "thank you". The respite has come to an end. We say, "Peace and blessings be upon you. Know that you are appreciated beyond words".

A concern often lifted up in the media is so many people die alone. No one should ever have to die alone. I can tell you nurses understand this. Whenever possible, a nurse will sit with a patient who is actively dying so the patient does not die alone. The nurse uses her/his tablet or cell phone or EPIC program or whatever tool is available to continue to monitor other patients for which the nurse is responsible. Nurse colleagues provide care as directed electronically. Each nurse knows the roles will be reversed, maybe even during that very shift. They do what they do because their profession is about caring, and new challenges require adaptations in responding and caring. Our chaplains' hearts swell with pride and love and awe as we watch nurses step in to the gap when we cannot be present in these times.

We have found that our trust in God, our faith in God, our love of God and our deep, heartfelt compassion for all of God's people trump theological differences. Consent forms are made available for families and/or patients to sign which allow us to engage in some rites and sacraments for families and patients that we otherwise might not be able to do... from a doctrinal perspective. We cling to the God who is love and compassionate and forgiving and grace-filled. We all are the better for it.

We learn of some faith communities who designate one among their midst to be the coronavirus priest/rabbi/pastor/imam. The individual lives an ongoing life in quarantine and/or isolation so she/he is able to go to the medical facility or nursing facility or assisted living facility on a moment's notice to offer prayer, encouragement, compassionate understanding, a gentle touch. We give thanks to God for such dedicated individuals.

It matters not if we are chaplains in a big hospital in a big city or a chaplain in a small hospital in a small town or remote part of the world, the challenges are the same: We find ways to live with the frustrations generated by the pandemic while providing compassionate care to patients, families, and medical staff and colleagues.

Tim Morrison, DMin, ND is a retired hospital chaplain and resides with his wife in Akron, Ohio. He is also a writing coach. Tim interviewed numerous chaplains from across the United States in creating this reflection.

MARIE L. MAY

I WOKE UP TODAY...
AND REALIZED MY LIFE IS BEAUTIFUL

Amid isolation, tragedy, medical mania, loss in abundance, misdirection, uncertainty, masquerading news at the forefront, 2020 has been a most bizarre year indeed.

It makes it easy to miss the delightful things happening in life all around you, large or small. But I woke up today... Every day is a new day, for a new beginning. Can you see? It is a matter of perspective. This year has taken its toll on me.

Brokenhearted is an understatement. The loss of my dearest friend. I am happy to have had so many years of marvelous memories. Memories of happy times that many people will never experience in life. What a blessing, right? A blessing undeniably, to have friends and family to love and to love me.

I woke up today...

Almost one million people did not. In the stillness, I hear from God. My 12th day of quarantine, from dreaded COVID-19. Defeating the diagnosis, surviving the sickness, praising my Higher Power and focusing on the future. Choosing not to feed energy into negativity, but to focus on the now to seek positivity.

Looking out of the window at children playing on the sidewalk, masked in the mindfulness of protection. Muffled laughs and giggles, finding happiness in the helplessness of what they cannot control. Continuing to live life because that is all they know.

Eyes aimed to the sky as a bird lands on the rooftop. I am in awe of its flawless flight and colorful quills. Oblivious of the world's plight, he takes off in flight, once again to rise, rise above it all.

Despite the turmoil of the world, the trees sway with the wind. Rooted in strength and longevity. The flowers continue to bloom. Vibrant expressions of my labor and creativity. Fragrant scents that I will smell once again.

I woke up today…

Staying connected through apps and social media, so that we are alone together. What an expression, right? I see my beautiful grandchildren's faces and innocent smiles, bringing the hope of many tomorrows. Air hugs and kisses, wonderful thoughts and wishes.

Working from home to make a difference in the lives of others. Being fortunate to have a career that allows me to live my life purpose. To help the helpless, feed the hungry, shelter the homeless, clothe the ragged and preserve the environment. To pay it forward, even when life sends you catapulting backwards.

Did I mention that I woke up today? Every day is a new day, for a new beginning. Can you see? Come and choose to carry on with me. Choose happiness and hope, love and light, purpose and peace, faith over fear, revive and renew.

Life is beautiful…

Marie L. May, new scintillating author, creating non-fiction genres that will uplift, inspire and heal the spirit. My works will bring thought provoking content to all readers through laughter, tears, turns and twists. Be bold, be beautiful and be blessed!

ANN BRADLEY

WHAT I'VE LEARNED OF BRAVERY

I've been called some iteration of brave or (my personal favorite) inspirational for as long as I can remember, as if just by existing I had undergone some epic hero's journey. It never fit for me, even though I understood why they said it. For many, I was the first young person in a wheelchair they'd seen, the first to go unaccompanied to a store, go away to college, or (*gasp*) pack up and fly to a country she'd never been to and live there for a year. For me, it's just life. I don't know how else to live it. Now, with COVID, I'm much more sedentary. I don't go out anywhere, and still, within the last week or so, I've been called brave. Just like when I was a child, I earned the moniker by breathing, or smiling, or some combination of the two.

My twin brother was honestly brave. With no use of his arms or legs, no way to even completely control the movement of his eyes, Tom dared to dream. He wrote stories, and gave beautiful speeches he had to memorize because his body didn't allow him the luxury of physically being able to read. He didn't care about the slur in his speech, or his physical differences brought on by cerebral palsy. He charmed everyone and lived his life as though there were no limitations. Tom died unexpectedly six years ago of pneumonia. He's been on my mind a lot in this time of COVID. He was on a ventilator, purple and silent, chest rising and falling mechanically for days as I clung to the hope that I lived in some sort of teen movie where if I gave him a good enough pep talk, he would come back to us. This shouldn't be news to anyone, but those movies lie. Or I'm not very good at inspirational speeches. The jury is out.

It wasn't bravery that kept me going in those weeks and months after Tom died, it was necessity with a dash of Irish stoicism. It's hard for me now to see images of people on ventilators. I'm transported as though no time has passed. I can hear the machine hiss. I know what a body looks like when it's been deprived of oxygen. Worse, I know the feeling when hope plummets along with your stomach, and you realize that whatever path you thought life was taking is no longer going to be. This might not seem very life-affirming, but I've learned a bit in these six years and in this time of quarantine. Despite all odds, trauma, loss, hopelessness and clawing anxiety, we have an incredible capacity to overcome.

Tom lived this. He didn't live long, nor did he leave some lasting mark on the world at large, just me, my family, and his friends. But that's enough. He's my inspiration, though I never told him that. He was living his life the only way he knew how. That's what we're all doing. In this world that seems like it's against us, we're taking a moment to create, or engage, or make bold moves we didn't think we had the daring to. We're diving in, reading a speech from memory; and our deviations, our mistakes, are likely even more beautiful than what we had written on the page.

Life is always uncertain; the difference is that we have a worldwide virus to remind us of that now. So, I think of Tom and his perseverance at the same time as I think of the tragedy of his short life. His memory, much like the moment we're living through now, is bittersweet. Like those days six years ago, we'll never forget this time. It won't always be positive. There might be loss or pain, economic hardship and widespread uncertainty, but there is also potential to seize this moment, do something beautiful, daring or unexpected. We can be brave, maybe even inspirational.

I love writing, even if it's only for myself. In normal times, I also love to travel, but currently spend quite a bit of time lounging on the couch with my dog.

KIMBERLE UNGER

HEADLINES

"Local woman spends birthday in emergency room. Her gift? A $5,000 panic attack."

That's me. I'm the local resident. And yes, unfortunately, I did spend my birthday in an emergency room. On April 25th, I was a 36-year-old woman experiencing shortness of breath and chest pain. I walked into my local emergency department at 11:40 that night and turned 37 twenty minutes later. The x-ray technician was the first one to wish me happy birthday after verifying my patient information. On a planet full of x-ray technicians, he had to have been the most miserable of them all. His voice was flat, devoid of any enthusiasm. In fact, the only emotion I heard in his voice that night is when he asked if I was pregnant before he took his x-ray. I insisted that I was not. And yes, I was absolutely certain. How can I be so certain? Because I'd had surgery to ensure my answer to questions like his would always be "no." He didn't believe me, and tossed a lead blanket on my abdomen because—his words—"I don't trust you women."

"Sour-faced medical professional doubles patient's depression after insulting the entire female sex."

The real insult came a few days later when I noticed they charged $100 for a pregnancy test. I could probably write a headline that points out that there's no shortage of reliable, readily available tests for less than $20, but I won't.

A headline I would write, however, would read something like:

"Woman with 20+ years experience being mentally ill still manages to mistake panic attack for cardiac emergency."

My doctor was much kinder than his colleagues. I'm thankful for his bedside manner and for his thoroughness, but I admit — I was embarrassed I didn't recognize a panic attack when I had one. My doctor didn't see someone who should have managed their mental illness better. He reassured me I was right in coming, and that I was by no means alone. There'd been a sudden influx of patients like me, he said. And the longer the pandemic went on, and the more socially isolated people became, the more mental health related visits he'd see. However, I know enough about mental illness (see: 20+ years experience) to catch the edge in his voice, and I heard what he wasn't saying. I read those headlines every day.

"Father of 3 succumbs to drug addiction; family cites job loss from pandemic."

"Medical examiner declares death of 12-year-old result of suicide by hanging."

"Missing woman found dead; suicide note reads: 'I feel so alone.'"

These headlines haunt me. Suicide is the silent consequence of living in a world that's never been so broken. I've never downplayed the seriousness of COVID-19 itself. It's terrifying to think that a mere virus could spread throughout the world so quickly. And in order to flatten the curve, businesses were forced to close, and people lost their jobs and their livelihoods. The economy suffered, and along with it, individuals and their families. Food pantries ran dry, and the unemployment website crashed because so many people applied at once. Hospitals were overwhelmed. Schools shut down. Churches suspended services. Important occasions were postponed or streamed online. Wildfires blazed out of control and a category 4 hurricane battered our coastlines. And in the midst of this, racial tensions are at an all-time high and politics have never been more divisive.

Because I am a now 37-year-old woman with 20+ years experience being mentally ill, I have always been more in tune with the needs of those in the mental health community, and maybe I tend to notice headlines regarding suicide and drug addiction more than most. But never, not even once, have I read a headline from mainstream media regarding this silent consequence of COVID. I've even posed my concern over the pandemic's impact on mental health with a friend. I was told that in order to save lives, lockdowns and quarantines must continue — suicide was just an "unfortunate consequence".

If suicide and self-harm is an unfortunate consequence of the pandemic, it is a result of mental illness being a silent disease to begin with. No one likes to talk about it, and if we can't discuss it, how are we going to address the problem? Now is the time for that to change. Everyone feels the weight of the world on our shoulders, one way or another. How can we not when so much is going on around us?

Eliminating stigma surrounding mental illnesses and making it easier to access the necessary care will take time, but there's something we can do now in order to improve our outlook. Do yourself a favor — log out of social media, turn off the news, and write your own headlines. Even in a broken world, there is good yet to be found. Here are some of my own headlines:

"Daughter rejoices after both parents found to be cancer free and celebrates their 40th anniversary."

"Unemployed writer finds time to finish book."

"Cat enthusiast befriends feral colony at local gas station."

"Quarantine & Quartets: Lazy musician rediscovers violin."

I've seen close friends become parents. I've seen people who had given up on love find their soul mates. I've had friends start new business ventures, and others have used their time to volunteer at animal shelters and other places. Good news is there; we just have to look for it. Don't forget— we are in this together.

And for those who might be like me and struggle with dark thoughts or feel that leaden weight of anxiety on their hearts, I say:

You may not realize it now, but you will emerge from this darkness, and you will feel the sun shine on your face again. You are stronger than you know. Don't give up. I *see* you. You matter to *me*.

Lover of the English language, history, art and playing violin, poorly. Established feline aficionado and connoisseur of humor. Resides in Charleston, South Carolina, but will always sound Minnesotan. Dreams of living in Australia. I love kangaroos.

DEBORAH H. BARBARA

WHEN THE WORLD FELL ILL

Two thousand and twenty the whole world went mad
A viral pandemic the worst one we've had,
Every country shut borders but it was too late
The virus had easily slipped through the gate.
The whole world in panic we were sent to our rooms
It was to defend the essentials, it's not over so soon.
The hospitals packed doing all that they can
Not one simple cure it was different than planned
The symptoms keep changing but what can they do
The whole world collapsed because of a flu!

While this keeps on going, those sent to their room
Begin an old fight because black lives matter too!
They are not wrong the system does need rebuilding
But if only they could remember to keep up the shielding.
As happens with arguments everyone wants their say
I just wish they looked to history it can show us the way.
Yes there is lots to do but stay in and be safe
The virus is killing us more each passing day.
The media tries to help, yet it muddies the choice
Political bias and riots accursed, the movement lost its
voice.

While this all ensued you feel surely we lost
But hope springs eternal no matter the cost
For while we are trapped inside of our home
Mother nature repaired some of the damage we've done
Although times were strange undoubtedly true

It gave us a chance to refocus anew,
While socially distancing we showed how we care
Putting rainbows in windows, sending what we could
share
We helped out our neighbours and families too
Our true human nature had a chance to shine through

We waved to our loved ones, sent friends a surprise
We found ways to connect using our tech and device
And our love for each other was stronger than hate
So while it was strange we all remember the date
For the whole world fell ill and brought about change
Not all change is bad and it's time we rearrange.
So history of the future look back and take note
The smarter we are the more stupid we vote.
I pray we all learn from the experience we shared
When the whole world fell ill and we ALL CARED.

*Deborah H. Barbara is a UK poet of little renown. I wish everyone well in
these tough times.*

BRIAN WEBB

❧

THE UBIQUITY OF HOPE

Six million. That is the figure of our current COVID-19 cases this last day in August. This has been a very cruel summer. No one is paying attention to social distancing measures. Fall is the time when school returns to session. We do not know how we can get our students to attend school safely. Mostly there has been talk of implementing an online program, yet that does not necessarily work for children with special needs. Or any child for that matter. The anxiety level in this country is off the charts. COVID has changed the game.

Besides this invisible enemy that can bring down nations, the civil unrest in this nation has reached a boiling point. When this virus began spreading in this country and affecting certain parts of America like Louisiana, Senator Bill Cassidy of Louisiana was questioned by NPR Morning Edition host David Green about the rise of infection in Senator Cassidy's State. Then a question was asked, "What about systemic racism?" The Senator was stunned and blew off the question by stating that the virus affects people severely with secondary conditions that communities of color are facing. Then, like a match thrown on an open tank of gasoline, the murders of George Floyd, Breonna Taylor, and the non-fatal shooting of Jacob Blake by white police officers has ignited the country in protests and riots.

To make matters even worse, it seems that the world is screaming to help her! With the pandemic we have also suffered numerous natural disasters. Northern California with its rising fire count. Hurricanes in the South are leaving a trail of destruction. Here in Iowa, this state suffered a land hurricane. At the beginning of the year there were bushfires in Australia. Devastating floods in Indonesia and India. Earthquakes in Turkey, the Caribbean, China, Iran, Russia, Philippines and India. A volcano erupts in the Philippines and locusts swarm in East Africa, India and Asia. Is Mother Nature trying to tell us something?

And if that is not enough, the global economy took a severe impact. Like being slapped in the face after the Great Recession, the virus has brought this country and world to its knees. I have a friend who once told me that we live in a service economy and this economy has been greatly affected. Most of the jobs in this country are service based: restaurant, retail, gyms, salons, barber shops; who around the first week of March shut their doors without any knowledge of when these stores would reopen. People working in close quarters were becoming ill. This virus has reached biblical proportions and the virus seemed to not end with this chaos that it was causing. But I have hope. Here is why.

My name is Brian Webb and I am a brain injury survivor. My trauma happened a week and a day after I graduated from college. A freak accident that no one would predict: a blood vessel in the back of my head became clotted and nearly ruptured, destroying the aspirations I set for myself. After spending two months in the hospital and moving back home to recover, the life I once knew was suddenly over. I could not work in the field of my choosing. I had to take time to heal. I really could not do anything except work in a grocery store or a retail establishment which I have done both. This became a hell for me. I found the light at the end of the tunnel, and that light is my fitness routine.

Four years later, in the fall of 2002, I began a membership with World's Gym in Cincinnati. I loved it! I fell in love with the exercises that would eventually challenge my body and changed my life for the better. I started to become fit. Over the years I have learned that exercise has become my best friend. People come and go, flings happen, relationships with parents or loved ones fade or pass on. I grade myself on whether I have a good workout that day. I got into running around 2004, since I need to be my own advocate for head injury. I run because I can, and have completed 20 half marathons and five full marathons. I discovered something else, exercise is good for my brain. According to the University of Cambridge, aerobic activity helps to grow gray matter in your brain. I started the long road of healing myself.

Exercise plus nutrition helps my head. The foods I eat help me to grow and to heal. Certain foods help my brain like fish; and anything that ends with berry like blueberry, raspberry, etc. helps prevent Alzheimer's and possibly dementia. The final ingredient in helping me is to get quiet. Turn everything off and get quiet for ten minutes twice a day. Once in the morning and once before I go to bed. This mindful meditation can help take me from this world to a world of utter peace and stillness.

The Dali Lama said in an issue of TIME magazine, "We need to look at the coronavirus with compassion." The book of Isaiah in the Bible reflects this idea in verse 43:19 where Isaiah's narrative quoted God on the prophecy of the tired, worn out history of His nation by stating, "Forget the former things; do not dwell on the past. See, I am doing a new thing! Now it springs up, do you not perceive it?" Again, is Mother Nature trying to tell us something? Are we going to become aware? We need to approach life differently. We need to look at our world like a hurt child. And we need to take care of ourselves. What gives me much solace, is looking at all the medals and plaques that I have earned since my brain injury. The awards I received after running

and finishing marathons. This gives me hope, and with hope
I have everything!

*My name is Brian Webb, I am a speaker, writer, health nut! Certified
personal trainer, speech mentor, running coach, photographer, traveler
and adventurer.*

MERSHON NIESNER

How Growing Up Without a Mother — and Other Life Changes — Helped Me Adapt to a Pandemic and Reclaim Joy

It is not the strongest of the species that survives, not the most intelligent. It is the one that is most adaptable to change. Charles Darwin, English naturalist, geologist, and biologist

Right now, as we experience the effects of an ongoing global pandemic, the challenge to become this person Darwin writes about, the one who is "most adaptable to change", is a constant. Older people, and those with underlying conditions, are adapting to a life of isolation. Those who are considered essential workers are adapting to working in potentially unsafe environments. We're all adapting to an unknown future.

Students and parents are making difficult choices about school as they evaluate in-person learning and/or virtual education. Special needs children, children who depend on meals at school, and children living in unsafe home environments are particularly impacted and may not have the capacity to adapt.

When The Rug Was Pulled Out

At the beginning of the pandemic, I felt the rug had been pulled out from under me. I'm a 75-year-old, very active — now isolated — woman who misses her past life.

However, with no kids to educate, no business to lose, good health, and isolating with a kind husband, I'm counting my blessings. Even with these positives, I spent the early months mourning my losses—a long-planned cruise, a family reunion/75th birthday party, summer with my grandchildren, an in-person book tour.

My History

Three dramatic life experiences taught me how to adapt to this pandemic.

1.   I first learned how to adapt to sudden and unprecedented change when my 34-year-old mother died and left my dad and I alone. I was eight.

2.   The second lesson was finding myself divorced after 25 years of marriage. I had to adapt to the challenges and insecurities of being a self-employed, single mother of three.

3.   Lesson three came when, at 55, after only ten months of marriage, I suddenly became a widow when my 53-year-old husband literally dropped dead of a heart attack.

I've had a lifetime to learn resilience, perseverance, and how to quickly adapt to change.

When COVID-19 closed us down in mid-March, I was about to publish *Mom's Gone, Now What?*; a book that details ten steps to help daughters move forward after loss. At first, I didn't make the connection to the sense of loss I was feeling due to the pandemic, and the advice I had spent three years researching and writing about. However, after a few weeks, I started tapping into six of the ten steps from my book.

Six Steps That Helped Me Adapt to Change – And Can Help You Too

1. Get Creative

As a child, I watched my dad model how creativity heals. As a single parent at 36, he found respite by creating on a wood lathe. This hobby not only helped him get through losing his young wife, it served him years later when his second wife died. Creative endeavors soothe me too. Today, I cook, paint, color, and write to give my life focus and joy.

2. Help Others

As a teenager without a mother, I found meaning in volunteering at a Veterans Hospital. Helping others helps me avoid the "why me?" question. I've found that simple acts of kindness such as dropping off cookies or making a phone call to an isolated friend helps keep me out of the doldrums.

3. Reach Out for Help

Many people who have experienced significant loss turn to therapy, counseling, or grief groups to help them heal. My losses due to COVID are minor in comparison to the loss of a loved one. Even so, I'm finding solace in reaching out to others when I'm feeling down. Even a quick text can be therapeutic.

4. Stay Mentally, Physically, Spiritually Healthy

The doors to my church are closed, my gym membership is canceled, my in-person social network is gone. I had to learn to find satisfaction in seeing friends and family on Zoom and exercise at home. At first virtual church felt stale and uninviting. Lately, I started singing along with the person on screen and find myself engaged in the service. Most Sunday services bring me to tears (the good kind) just as they did in the church building.

5. Accept the Hand You're Dealt

To me, adaptability is knowing how to make lemonade out of lemons so I asked myself, "How can I use this situation to my advantage?" As I contemplated how to do a book tour, meet with groups, and make presentations, Zoom proved to be my lemonade. I'm also taking advantage of the free webinars experts are producing in lieu of conferences. I'm learning to accept the hand I was dealt.

6. Tell Your Story

To help us regain our equilibrium, we need to tell and retell our COVID stories. We're sharing what we're missing, what we're looking forward to, and affirming our realization about what is really important. In 2017, after Hurricane Irma hit my area, it was all we talked about for weeks, even months. COVID is like that. Telling our stories helps to relieve some of the fear and anxiety. We bond over our common experience. Storytelling is critical in our healing and adaptation to a new reality.

What I Know to Be True

I know from past experience that I am resilient. As Darwin said, I will survive and thrive because I know how to adapt. You can too as you remind yourself of your past life experiences and how you coped. How was your ability to adapt in the past serving you now? What steps will you take to thrive in this season of change?

Mershon Niesner is a Certified Life Coach and author of Mom's Gone, Now What? Ten Steps to Help Daughters Move Forward After Mother Loss. *She is a Certified Life Coach, retired social worker, and newspaper columnist. In her book, Mershon shares her own early loss story along with information from over 50 daughters who experienced young adult loss, abandonment, homicide, or Alzheimer's loss.*

KATIE DEBONVILLE

GUIDELINES

"Not feeling up to our chat today."

That text was the first indication that something was wrong. It was March and I'd just completed nine days of being quarantined. It felt like forever since I'd seen anyone, so my friend and I decided we'd have Sunday evening virtual drinks.

Further texts revealed that he was exhibiting the early signs of COVID-19. Suddenly missing out on a drink seemed both terribly unimportant and terrifically significant. Just one more sign that normal didn't exist anymore.

I don't scare easily. I worry, so I combat that with a plan. I use humor as a defense mechanism when exploring the truth seems inconvenient, for lack of a better term. But feeling scared? That's admitting you don't have a plan. That's harder to fight.

I was scared.

Not for me, but for him. It was early in the game; the direction of the virus was so much more of an unknown than it is now. Yes, more people were surviving it than not, but the news only covered the tragedies, the stories of the people who went into the hospital alone, armed with a cell phone to connect them to their people on the outside, and didn't leave. Needless to say, he was scared too.

We made a plan. Guidelines, we called them. We would text daily, even if it was just a two-text exchange confirming the fact that we were both still present. We would tell the truth, even if it sucked. And we would somehow help get each other through this patch of uncharted territory.

If I have two superpowers, they are my ability to be relentlessly optimistic in the face of adversity, and my ability to project relentless optimism. In other words, to make it and to fake it. Over the next few weeks, I did far more faking than making. Knowing that someone you care about is suffering, and not being able to do anything about it – especially when your natural inclination is to DO – is hard. The feeling of being scared never really left me during that time. It was always there, under the surface, ready to pop back up just when you'd convinced yourself that it was okay to let your breath out – or in my friend's case, take your breath in. Like the progression of the disease itself – an analogy I hesitate to make because fighting fear is so much easier than fighting COVID-19 – there were extreme highs and lows. Raucous laughter and unanticipated tears. "This is going to be fine" and "What if…?"

This story has a happy ending, inasmuch as there are happy endings these days. My friend has recovered. We eventually enjoyed the virtual drink we'd planned, and it was one of the best glasses of wine I've ever had – and in the past fifteen weeks, I've had my share of actual glasses of wine in virtual situations!

But the scared feeling hasn't completely gone away. We're still living in quarantine. The world remains a mess, one that has expanded well beyond the global pandemic that kickstarted this clusterfuck not that long ago. And there's no sign that the situation is going to end anytime soon.

Thank god for the friends who help us get through whatever the world throws at us. Fear is overcome by friendship.

Katie DeBonville is a professional arts fundraiser who lives in Boston. In addition to writing, which she has done more frequently during the pandemic, her interests include going to concerts, reading, and spending time with friends.

CAREER &
LIFE SHIFTS

SCOTT CURRY

❧

CIRCUMSTANTIAL NORMAL

Indeed our environment and circumstances shape us in many ways, but it is our internal resolve and tenacity for 'better' that drives us to embrace them and make a change. I was in a great job for twelve years, one that I thought that I would retire from, but due to the COVID-19 economic pandemic my employer made lay-offs and my last day was May 9, 2020.

The coronavirus pandemic forced myself and American society to take stock in ourselves, our loved ones, and re-evaluate how we spend our time and what's important to us.

Humans have a deep-seated desire to establish a comfortability and 'normal' that is our own. However, we admire people that are comfortable living outside of their comfort zone, thriving in the unknown, living in the moment, and optimizing their circumstances as best they can.

I found myself in this position and proceeded to reinvent my work/life balance by spending time on only things I loved. It's amazing how you can change your circumstances by only operating from a place of love.

I've read a lot of books, carved a multicultural totem pole, written stories, edited short films, took lots of walks and bike rides with my son, went sailing, and most importantly spent quality time with my family.

All throughout the pandemic I kept hearing people using the phrase this is the 'new normal'.

To me, describing something as 'normal' has always been fairly ambiguous, much like the word 'weird', and has not had a place in my vernacular. There is no 'new normal' and any attempt to define one is to put oneself in an infinite cycle of unrest and survival.

Americans have a culturally ingrained belief for the right to 'the pursuit of happiness'. Instead of pursuing it, I simply made the choice to just be happy.

I find it helpful to measure aspects of my life on a scale of surviving to thriving. Whether it's my marriage, raising our son, my work, my relationships, or my hobbies, it helps me measure how I feel about things and to proceed in evolving accordingly.

Time itself is an invention and there is only the now. The circumstances that you're in right at this moment. What actions and words you choose to change your circumstances, to move toward thriving, that's all up to you.

Right now.

Those that believe in the power of intention and action can attest to the disbelief in 'normal'. Normal and life should never be used in the same sentence, unless to say they don't belong in the same sentence.

If you're unhappy with your circumstances, don't accept them as normal; see them as building blocks upon which to grow and shape the life you feel you need to live in order to be the best you.

Changing your circumstances begins with accepting you can indeed change them, that you can indeed live a happy and fulfilling life.

A little in a day, a lot in a week, a bunch in a month. Start being what you want to be at this very moment. I know it works.

Now get to work and start thriving.

Scott Curry is an insatiably optimistic renaissance man that lives in Shaker Heights, OH with his wife Tina, son Åsmund, and dogs Saoirse and Santtu. He loves designing brands and campaigns, writing on a ROYAL typewriter while listening to classical music on vinyl, and imagining bedtime stories with his son. He's worked with iconic brands around the world including Arnold Palmer, Olympics, Fashion Week, and numerous non-profit initiatives.

Image from Scott Curry

COVID SILVER LININGS REFLECTION

I work from home (I have my own business), so working remotely and digitally is nothing new to me, and I didn't really have to make any adjustments because of COVID. Luckily, my business continued as it had before the shutdown, so even from that perspective, work didn't really feel any different to me.

Personally though, was an ENTIRELY different matter. I am a very social person... a 'hugger'... and being part of something (belonging) is really important to me. And, no surprise, my love language is physical touch, so being single with no children and the nearest family a 6-hour drive away was HARD.

Like many people, I became depressed. I didn't know what to do with myself, and even though I was 'used' to living alone, and working from home, if *felt* different. Knowing that I couldn't go out and find ways to connect with people and find outlets for my social nature was brutal.

Being 'forced' to be alone with yourself is an interesting experience. I don't think we realize how little most people actually take the time to really, truly get alone with ourselves.

It's scary. That means I might have to face thoughts and demons I thought I had successfully pushed to the deepest darkest corners of my mind, there to dwell in silence for all eternity. That I might have to come face to face with some of those unflattering or negative beliefs I have held about myself – you know, the ones that aren't true and don't serve you any more... but you hang onto them anyway because they keep you "safe"?

In the first six weeks, I had the television on ALL the time. I needed the sound, the company, the distraction. I worked with the television on, I sat in front of the television for dinner and until I went to bed. Like so many of us, I binge-watched television shows, romantic movies, comedies, you name it! Anything to keep me from having to face myself.

Silence was VERY uncomfortable.

But then, something happened... I began to get comfortable with being with myself. I actually took some time for introspection. I turned off the television and intentionally explored some of those darker corners of my mind. I reached out to friends and family, instead of waiting for them to reach out to me. I had virtual happy hours, and video chats... and one day, I realized I hadn't had the TV on all day. I discovered that I *liked* myself. That being alone with myself was really very freeing and very valuable time that we don't get much these days.

Getting to know myself better helped me solidify what I really want to do with my business. What my dreams are for my life. It helped me define what "success" really means to me – not what the world tells me it's supposed to look like. It helped me reconnect with an old friend and create a collaboration group, which led to a new product... which is totally in line with what I really want my work to be about.

I traded television for audiobooks and podcasts by people who were doing what I wanted to do or had knowledge that could help me get there. I created a vision board for my future, and started speaking into what it will be like... envisioning my ideal day, the travels I will go on, the people I will work and spend time with. Without the 'noise' of everyday life, things became crystal clear. Having this time of quiet allows me to really anchor in this new knowledge and vision, without distraction.

I chose not to watch the news... not to get sucked into the fear and misinformation that is so rampant these days. I stay informed, but that's all.

What began as a lonely, scary time has turned into an internal awakening of sorts, bringing me closer to what I want for my life. Even in the midst of the turmoil, I find I am grateful for the opportunity, and for the silence.

With a life-long desire to help others and be a catalyst for growth, Cami built a service-based business while living in Colorado. Established in 1993, she worked with clients on business operations development, business plan writing, and financial controls. Cami's clients look to her to provide leadership as well as consulting services to help support their business needs.

MARK SCHNEIDER

MY ~~SILVER~~ GOLD LINING

Tumultuous times always give birth to fresh perspectives and silver linings. I'm extraordinarily thankful that the Pandemic brought me back to my past and improved my quality of life today. Let me briefly explain:

I was born with an incredible gift — a crazy creative mind. My wild imagination fueled a storybook marketing career and dominated my life until my "lifequake" occurred. Coined by The New York Times writer Bruce Feiler, a "lifequake" [paraphrased] is a series of life-altering events that collide and flip your world upside down. My lifequake shook my soul, my confidence, and my life. Unbeknownst to me, the experience altered the fabric of my creative being. I did not realize how damaging my actions were until...

THE PANDEMIC DELIVERED THE ULTIMATE WAKEUP CALL

Being quarantined, I took a deep dive into me for the first time in eons and had revelations galore:

As I flew up the career ladder and became a business leader, my creative skills slowly but steadily started to erode. Unknowingly, I focused on the bottom line at the expense of "creative excellence." Short-term, it paid off handsomely. It eventually took a significant toll on my career.

When opportunities arose to escape corporate and lead startups, I was ecstatic. I believed it would provide the best of both worlds: do what I love and become wealthy. What

I didn't realize is that the majority of startup founders do not understand marketing. The majority believe, "My genius idea will sell itself."

Therefore, big ideas, smart strategies, and extraordinary creative solutions — the things I'm most passionate about and work the best — were not respected. So, my daily journey was focused 100% on business: writing marketing decks, investor decks, pitch presentations decks, data analysis summaries, and engaging in endless pitches.

Piggybacking on the above, I unconsciously surrounded myself with businesspeople, not creative folks.

Piggybacking on the piggyback, I attended business events instead of art museums; I listened to business books instead of music. Even my favorite morning ritual changed: instead of starting the day with a cup of coffee and my beloved sports section, I read business journals.

"My revelations continued to pick up steam. I uncovered illuminating sh*t about myself"

- I focused more on my clients' needs than my own wishes and goals
- I paid more attention to CPCs and CPLs than my own physical and mental health
- I shared more dinners with business associates than my family

Although I considered myself spiritual, I had little time for elements that nourish the creative soul: nature walks, Indy movies, meditation, and photography

"As I explored life in the new normal, my vision was as bright and peaceful as the Caribbean. I knew my new normal life must resemble my distant past."

I'm happy to report that I've transformed back to my creative roots with aplomb:

- Daily work journeys are now creative driven

- I'm surrounding myself with creative folks
- Chemistry now defines who I collaborate with and walk away from
- Spirituality, exercise, and fun no longer take a back seat to work
- Making a difference in people's lives is paramount

DIVINE INTERVENTION INTERVENED

When starting anew, we all look for signs that we're on the right track. Thankfully, I received confirmation: A series of unconnected events serendipitously connected. I launched a new business that is driven by immersive storytelling and focused on impacting people's lives. Purpose and passion will hopefully transform the idea into a full-blown business.

In the meantime, my creative journey — part Deux — continues. Admittedly, I'm far from my peak. Proudly, I am many moons beyond where I was this past January.

MY LIFE IS NO LONGER A SERIES OF SPRINTS IN PURSUIT OF THE GOLDEN RING

I'm embracing the "life is a marathon" theory: I'm taking it "a step at a time, and a day at a time" doing what I do the best and love the most: create.

Like everyone else on earth, I wish COVID-19 never arrived, but it did. I'm extraordinarily thankful that a golden lining found me. I pray that more and more people find their silver — or gold — linings, too.

As a multi-media immersive storyteller, copywriter & content developer I have worked with over one-third of the Fortune 1000 and dozens of startups around the globe. As an executive creative director, I successfully launched two national creative divisions and held the role of CMO for a handful of startups.

ROBIN ROSE

CORONA SILVER LINING & AGEISM

I've been in the workforce since I was an entrepreneurial 12-year-old who found herself in need of earning income. From watering plants and taking care of animals while people were on vacation or filing for a local office, I always found a way to make money. Over the years, I've engaged in more career paths than any ten people I know. My belief has been there's always an opportunity, I just had to find it.

A year and a half ago, the real estate redevelopment project I was overseeing for two years, was sold before we began construction and I once again found myself in the job market. Today's market wants more clever resumes; certifications over experience; and younger, less expensive labor. After over 35 interviews, it became abundantly clear that my more-salt-than-pepper hair created a stigma of an 'older' person and it was my first real exposure to 'ageism'. I have more experience, excellent recommendations and a greater work ethic than your average millennial out there, but I'm over 60 and no one seemed to value that experience.

Thankfully, there was unemployment, but as you know, it only lasts for six months. Then the world got turned upside down with COVID-19. Now everyone was out of work and the government created the stimulus package and supplemental unemployment. On top of this, my mortgage and credit bills all got put on forbearance. Remarkably, I was in a position to capitalize on an opportunity to start a new career, one that I've always dreamed about; designing kitchens. Having designed many of my own kitchens and a few for others, I thought I'd be pretty good at doing it professionally, but I had many obstacles: 1. I needed someone to give me the opportunity; 2. They would have to hire me with little professional experience; 3. I needed flexibility to not have to worry about income to start.

So a miracle happened--all things conspired to make my dream come true. While renovating my daughter's kitchen, I hired a countertop supplier to install the tops. We got to talking and I asked if they were looking to hire a kitchen designer. Miraculously, he said they were currently looking for one and I should come speak to his partner. Two weeks later, I started working for them part-time, learning on the job what I didn't already know. While they weren't willing to pay me a salary while I learned, they were willing to pay me a commission.

Since my unemployment got renewed for an additional 13 weeks, I was able to work for free while I learned my new career and my employer was willing to give me the opportunity to prove myself and most importantly, they never even asked my age or seemed to care. While I still have a lot to learn, I'm on my way, having the time of my life helping other people create their dream kitchens.

Long-time real estate professional who has recently been gifted the opportunity to start a new career. Mother of three amazing daughters and a totally cool dog.

GUY GILCHRIST

LOOK FOR THE LESSON – THE GIFT

After being a syndicated Cartoonist, children's book author and illustrator - and being involved in daily production of animated television shows for four decades, I took to in-person Comicon appearances and Motivational Speaking tours quite happily a couple of years ago.

My career – which has included being Jim Henson's Cartoonist on The Muppets, Muppet Babies and Fraggle Rock, and writing and drawing such TV favorites as Looney Tunes, Tom and Jerry, Teenage Mutant Ninja Turtles, as well as 23 years writing and drawing the Nancy comic strip - had kept me at the drawing board for decades as all of the 70s, 80s, and 90s kids grew up! So, I was having a lovely time out on tour when the virus stopped all of that.

I certainly was going to miss all of the love and the smiles from the terrific people I was meeting!

I also felt helpless. I usually could find a way to make myself happy by making other people happy… But that had just been taken away from me.

Through Instagram, Dr Karen Tsai, Doctor of internal Medicine in Los Angeles, reached out to me and invited me to check out her organization DonatePPE.org.

Karen and her team, made up of people in the medical profession and volunteers, were finding protective equipment for Frontline workers all over the country while they were still at their jobs as doctors during the pandemic! I was absolutely blown away and I wanted to help.

I was invited to contribute coloring pages and drawings to brighten up the hospitals, and I was very grateful for the opportunity! I first drew Kermit, and other iconic characters I've worked on, wearing masks, washing their flippers, paws and claws, and social distancing. Then, I created some new original characters called PPE Pals to educate and entertain for future Charitable projects.

In difficult times, I always try to look for the lesson. The gift. There's always something. In this case… not being able to draw for anyone in person while being in isolation, gave me the opportunity to create brand new characters and reach many, many people that I would not have otherwise - while helping to raise money and awareness to provide protective equipment for our heroes on the front lines.

I realized I had a part to play. Drawing makes me happy. If it also makes a difference, I'm even happier.

Kindness Always, Guy

World-renowned, award-winning illustrator, author, comic strip artist, and songwriter, Guy Gilchrist is best known for his work on Jim Henson's MUPPETS *, as well as* Teenage Ninja Turtles, Tom & Jerry, The Pink Panther, and Nancy. *His iconic* Muppets *artwork is enshrined in the Smithsonian Institute. He has written 42 children's books and won Reuben and Children's Choice Awards for his work.*

Artwork by Guy Gilchrist

JONAH SIMCHA CHAIM MUSKAT-BROWN

THE NEED FOR TEMPORARY DWELLINGS

We often talk about there being things in life that are
beyond our realm of human reason or that we don't agree
with because we can't relate to them. We also know that
there are events and experiences in life that we will never
comprehend ever, for, in the words of the Prophet, Isaiah,
God's ways are not our ways nor are His thoughts our
thoughts. But these conversations tend to focus on, and
create, negative vibes – such as why the Holocaust, or racism,
or cancer, or COVID. If we can somehow come to terms
with possibly never fully understanding the causes for evil,
why can't we also appreciate that joy doesn't always need
a justification, as well? Why do we always wait for reasons
to be happy...as if it's wrong to be happy unless something
particular transpires that warrants that joy? Why can't we
just dance at random, or smile, or sing? And, perhaps, if we
cultivate the courage to choose joy for no apparent reason,
maybe we'll be blessed all the more so with actual reasons
to celebrate.

Over the years, I've learned that there are two basic
structures of reality, and a distinct type of individual who
inhabits each. The first is that of a building. This structure is
permanent and built upon a solid foundation of many hours
of investment and hard work. True, it could be demolished,
but most likely it'll survive the harsh weathers and withstand
many years. The second is that of a tent. A tent, by definition,
is temporary. It's a shelter we erect when we don't intend to

stay somewhere for very long and usually doesn't take much time or skills to set up. Its foundation isn't nearly as strong as that of a building nor can it withstand the elements.

And yet, how many of us have time, money, or skills to invest in building buildings? We all have busy lives – whether that's supporting our own needs or the additional needs of family members. We have jobs, appointments, and projects to get done, and by the time we get through our daily tasks, how many of us actually have time for enjoyable pursuits or self-care? And really, even if we do find a few moments to steal in our day, do they even make a difference?

Meanwhile, how can we stay sane if we're always on the go and pitching tents for immediate and short-term usage? What if we're not the "building" type of people who can fully and properly invest in ourselves and our permanence?

Maybe it's because we try so hard – *and too hard*. Maybe it's because we plan and cloud our brains with justifications and details of the many when's, how's, and where's. There's so much chaos in our world and so much beyond what we can comprehend – and sometimes even just process. Sometimes what we need are those "tent moments"…the times in our busy days where we choose joy over confusion, mindfulness over busyness, kindness over strict-judgment. The times when we choose to dance in the rain, or lie down and roll through the grass, or the times we sing our favorite song at full volume because we're sure nobody's listening. They may be small moments in time and seem unworthy or superficial in our minds, but maybe that's just what we need. That 3 minutes we sneak into our afternoon to do a quick meditation; that 9 seconds we take to say a prayer; that smile we share with another; the phone call we make; those few pages we read in a book…

How much time do we spend thinking and planning that we don't actually get to enjoy those plans?

Most camps were either cancelled or immensely altered this past summer, but maybe that's irrelevant because in actuality, we can set up camp wherever we are and regardless of season. We may surprise ourselves by how rejuvenating and positively-lasting those temporary dwellings can be!

Jonah Simcha Chaim is a social worker, educator, and freelance author from Toronto, Canada. When not working in the field or behind his computer on a new piece of writing, he can be found in the forests on his mountain bike, in the backcountry bowls on his snowboard, or at the climbing gym or crag. He enjoys being creative, looking at the world upside down to make meaning out of it, and is a rebel against words like "normal" and "impossible."

EDWIN W. SMITH, CLC

COVID-19 SILVER LININGS

There is an interesting psychological concept referred to as a 'negativity bias' which suggests that we give much more weight or attention to negative news than positive or good news. Research results estimate that it takes 4 to 5 good incidences to overcome one negative incident.

It is for this reason that I put together this list of silver linings about the COVID-19 pandemic, which I posted on one of my blogs and some social media sites. While this list will not offset the volume of negativity and anxiety brought on by the coronavirus pandemic, this Opyrus LifeWrite Project seems to be a perfect place to share this list. Please enjoy and I hope these will at least partially offset the negative news and anxiety attributable to the Coronavirus pandemic.

- Telemedicine, which has been around for more than a decade, got a huge boost in usage and will finally be more accepted.
- There have been very few deaths from traffic accidents. Consequently, many insurance companies have issued nominal premium rebates or credits.
- The price of oil/gasoline plummeted due to the oversupply.

- People are eating more, presumably healthier, home-cooked meals.

- Interest rates are at record lows, though a double-edged sword.

- The AARP, other national organizations and many local communities have instituted community Wellness Checks for the elderly and others.

- There are some very inexpensive stocks to be had.

- Many families have been able to enjoy much more family time that they otherwise would have had time for.

- So far, over 99% of the people who contracted the COVID-19 virus have recovered, a far higher percentage than the MERS, SARS or Ebola viruses.

- Various and numerous acts of kindness for both friends and strangers abound (social capital).

- Employers are already and will be more open to remote or telecommuting work and such options will be more available moving forward.

- Dolphins appear to be thriving in the Sardinian city of Cagliari.

- Governments will be much better prepared to handle future pandemics.

- Air pollution has plummeted with carbon dioxide emissions down by up to 30% in quarantined metro areas around the world.

- The waters and canals in and around Venice, Italy are visibly clearer in the absence of boat traffic and tourists.

- A BBC story covered how the lockdown has been good for wildlife species of all kinds.

- There appears to be a newfound appreciation and respect for lower-wage 'essential' workers.

- Ditto for front-line healthcare professionals.

- Ditto for supply chain workers.

- Talking about supply chains: while resilient, we did discover weaknesses that need to be and will be corrected.

- Connection and interaction times have increased for both family and friends, albeit virtually.

- Parents are getting a better understanding of what teachers go through dealing with their children.

- Garages, kitchen pantries and drawers everywhere have been purged and reorganized.

- Churches, temples, and synagogues have learned how to stream their services and events. (My parish offered drive-up blessings recently.)

- K-12 schools and other educational institutions had an opportunity to evaluate their infrastructure and connectivity needs and shortcomings in real time and are making corrections.

- The timeline for vaccine research has been greatly accelerated.

- Many grocery stores are offering dedicated shopping hours for seniors and the disabled.

- People, especially many parents, have become more tech-savvy.

- Internet connectivity shortcomings and digital divide issues were uncovered.

- Many people have developed a higher level of mindfulness and self-awareness.

- More people have taken up breathing exercises and meditation to lower stress and anxiety.

- Animal shelter adoptions have skyrocketed in many areas with some shelters having been emptied out completely.

Mr. Smith enjoyed two successful careers, first as a rehabilitation counselor and then as an IT Program/Project Manager. After retiring from full-time work, he became a Certified Life Coach and Life Purpose coach and periodically worked as a consultant and freelance writer.

James A. Garland

❦

The Great Experiment vs. The Great Work

It is my presumption, that with self-governance comes a greater need to evolve both individually and collectively. If, for example, we base our expectations on distorted dogma of any religion passed down through various stages of oppression in the lifeline of human existence and interactions with others, that hammers disrespect for non-believers or practitioners of other religions, that is a dire formula for immeasurable consequences.

Since the fifties, when television first appeared on the scene, people's minds have been froth with conditional programming, on top of already cultural expectations from parents, parishioners and clergy, adults with good intention (perhaps); nevertheless, an overwhelming slew of programming started residing in the unconscious. A development that unwittingly is the collective that we're all living proof of. Advertisers using their will through this media press down the public's Will when desire for some product, be it a car, face cream, cereal, contrived semblance of strength, or whatever, supersedes their own conscious, rational thinking. Nothing is wrong with wanting better or to be and do better by improving circumstances in life, but problems occur when people base these desires only and extremely on the material, the external things rather than the inner work needed to stay ahead, or at the least, not fall behind advancements in technology. A powerful saying goes something like this; "When man's evolution is based on the external rather than the internal, great chaos will suffice the collective unconscious." We've come to expect only reactive responses in ourselves to anything, if not everything, that the external world presents to us. These are not gifts. We are responding to advertisers by buying their products on a whim or perhaps a plan is put in place that will shine lights when we are finally driving down the street in our new Infiniti Convertible. Or, as an archaic adage goes: "Keeping up with the Joneses." Sound familiar? Cellphones, however, have replaced the mere automobile in popularity and must haves, and their costs will surely supersede the auto industry too, someday.

The Great Experiment – America's experiment of self-governing requires even Greater work – The Great Work, which is the trajectory of prophets, mystics, altruism, and the like. Spiritually inclined folks work includes: questioning one's own action, one's thinking, responses and non-responses to the external world regardless of media persuasion; where did these actions or thoughts originate and what are they actually based on, truth or fallacy. "I was raised this way" no longer befits the 2020 vision of those who consider themselves 'woke'.

Jesus, the Buddha, and countless prophets of both genders understood the necessity of divining within, of leaving behind that which no longer served, of a need to serve. Seeing within the pre-consciousness and disrupting its sponge-like neighbor's suction of information and holding it encased in the unconscious action of all types is definitely something worth walking away from. Teachings of the sacred came from the internal work done by those less influenced by society and its peculiar norms, and more by a ceaseless prodding that comes from awakening the true self, and thus taking self-responsibility in reordering the internal chaos of emotions that have arranged themselves in distortion, both internally and externally. In other words, it's imperative that we turn the channel from within first. When "We the people, for the people, and by the people" understand our true self in connection to others and all things then, true self-governance will succeed and competition is thus nil, as we are all in this together. This is truly, the Great Experiment in the works.

However, when the pandemic erupted, naivete took hold. Maybe this will become the opportunity, a rude catalyst, for us humans finally making the connection, which is the interconnectedness of our species. We would finally admit this as Earth inhabitants and begin to undergo a major shift. Especially, since COVID-19 holds the heavyweight belt and with multiple blows, broadcast worldwide – brought the whole world to its knees. A true knock-out in the crudest sense.

During lockdown, the Pollyanna winds continued to wrestle my mind like a clinging moth battles a flame. We just weren't low enough. Were WE! The heavyweight champion of the world wasn't killing us fast enough, apparently. It took another knee to remind the collective of the darkness of the soul. How ignorance, hate, and anger have swerved an upper hand and merged as another crude champion worth defeating. Not merely one person, although with "great power comes a *greater responsibility*," nor a political force, police force, or another foe, like the virus and other climatic returns does the power lie, exclusively. We know the words to describe these emotional times and yet, we see them escape somewhere off into oblivion. They become useless. Words used to matter. Lives should always matter. The Soul *must* matter and once we individually, collectively, consciously, and determinedly set our sights on not mere repetitive, albeit begrudgingly, needed Revolutions, but rather an awakened approach to our Evolution as a species; then, the vibration of true healing will become the New norm and as with any aspiring opponent, training must become ritual.

My interest in writing probably goes back to the late Walter Cronkite. His voice and journalistic reporting while Mom cooked salmon patties with greasy onions and I was coloring at the kiddie table are forever the soil that supports this tree of ambition. May leaves of dreams forever wave in the listening winds.

RACHAEL MALTBIE

PANDEMIC URBEX: HOW PHOTOGRAPHY HELPED ME COPE WITH COVID-19

Once the pandemic hit, we were remanded to our homes to go through the five stages of grief for our former lives, either on our own or with close family. FOMO or 'fear of missing out' wasn't as much of a factor as it once was, as most people were home and in quarantine. For the first time, we were on a level playing field. Comparison — a creativity-killer — wasn't as prevalent. We started looking to ourselves, discovering who we were without all the noise that previously distracted us. The veil was lifted. Once Netflix outlived its novelty, and because we couldn't socialize in places like bars or concerts, we left their homes to be in nature, to discover the power of the sun and earth, to discover things like landmarks and preserves we'd driven past without a second though in our former lives.

Before the pandemic, photography was something I had thought I couldn't do. I had purchased a Canon DSLR camera when I had been a freelance journalist, so I'd have photos to accompany the articles I had written. I had used the DSLR's 'auto' setting. I had documented events, people, places, things. But my photographs had never been art.

At press events, I had been envious of the professional photographers with their fancy set-ups, light meters, and tripods. They scurried about to create shot after shot. They were so passionate. So driven. Never mind they were being paid for what they were doing. The pay didn't seem to be as important as getting just the right photo during magic hour (the hour after sunrise or before sunset). As a writer, I had found their behavior comical then; but now, I know I had been jealous. Photography felt overwhelming—I thought 'the eye' was something you were born with; you either had it or didn't have it—so I never tried. It wouldn't be until the pandemic hit that I realized photography was something I loved.

My love of Urbex—short for *urban exploration*—photography started during the transition from a normal social life to quarantine. It provided me a means to get out of the house and explore while maintaining social distancing. Just before the pandemic, I had worked the voting polls for the presidential primaries alongside some other Apple Valley locals. We had all day to talk, and during our down time, my cohorts discussed places they had visited by horse or 4x4, places like a rock circle, and old mines out by the dry lakebed. This conversation made me curious, and because I didn't have a horse or a 4x4, my husband and I instead visited places we could get to from the road, like the Victorville Jail and abandoned homes off route 66. I photographed every location, my addiction to urbex growing stronger every time. Then, after the pandemic hit, my husband and I were driving on back desert roads, partly out of boredom, and partly in an attempt to find stores with toilet paper when we came across another fascinating location, the abandoned housing section of what used to be George Air Force Base: an urbexer's paradise.

The abandoned world is a fascinating glimpse into the past through the lens of decay. I began my journey into this world on 'Atlas Obscura', a website full of articles, photos, and videos about the world's anomalous people, places and history. They have a map with the locations of all the local abandoned places and this map guided me, family and friends to locations all over southern California.

The process of researching, planning, exploring, photographing, and posting the pictures that are the rewards of my effort are what have kept me going during these uncertain times. For example, Stone Castle Powerhouse is a 100-year-old former hydroelectric powerhouse located on private property in the greater Los Angeles area. I first discovered it on Atlas Obscura and then drove out to the location early one morning. I spoke to the owner and we became friends. She allowed me access to the property for photographs and it was like being in a scene from *The Secret Garden* where the vines wrapped around the walls and threatened to consume the castle into oblivion at any second. I couldn't believe that such a historical marvel had been here all along, hidden behind trees in front of someone's house. I went back with my husband and some friends and they gawked just as I had when I saw it for the first time. It's this majesty I'd like to portray in my photographs.

Initially, I used an iPhone; and took an iPhone photography class to learn about lighting and composition, editing apps, and even an app that enables one to use manual camera settings with an iPhone. I've been taking a photography class on Udemy and have picked up another DSLR camera. My photos aren't the best yet, but that doesn't matter. I'm 'unplugged'. I'm free to create without the influence of others.

The beauty of photography is that 1,000 photographers can take a photo of the same thing but, with point of view and editing, not a single photo looks the same. Each photo tells its own story, and we need each and every one of those stories. When I look back on the pandemic, I don't want to remember the fear and the paranoia. I want to remember how we grieved for a former life and then created a new one in whatever way we knew how.

Rachael Maltbie is a writer, investigator and photographer who spends her days investigating claims, and her weekends exploring with her husband or nieces. She posts photos of the locations she's visited on her Instagram.

Rachel Maltbie: Abandoned Hospital at George Air Force Base

Rachel Maltbie: Abandoned Pendergast Motel in Ludlow, California

Rachel Maltbie: Abandoned Housing at Georgia Air Force Base

LAURIE DALY

SITTING IN DARKNESS, AWAITING THE LIGHT

As I sat in darkness listening to the wind howling outside, I found myself reflecting on the title of this piece, for it was not that long ago that it had a much different meaning in my life. Because, you see, it's the last week in August in South Louisiana, and Hurricane Laura was making landfall soon somewhere along the Gulf Coast. We prepare for these events here, but no one can prepare for the devastation that was imminent with a storm of this magnitude. It was out of our control. In these dark hours of the night, we knew that its effects would only be revealed when daylight broke. 2020 has been a year for the books, to say the least. It's the thing that most, if not all, of us can agree on, regardless of our life situations. In a world filled with chaos, confusion, fear, questions, divide, and strife, it's a somber thought that so many would wake up to yet even more devastation in their lives. Whether I would be one of those people remained to be seen. But despite this uncertainty, I found myself quiet inside. Peaceful, even. I made my way to the sofa closest to the nearest exit, held my sweet dog close, and somehow was able to fall asleep despite the noise outside.

When I awoke the following morning, Laura had passed. The brunt of it had hit to the west of me and if we could get through the next few hours and avoid the storm surge, then it looked like we were in the clear. With no electricity or means of information about what was going on around me, I could only hope and pray that everyone was safe and would find the strength to carry on. That has been a recurring theme of this year, and while it always is, it's a bit different when it's felt on the collective level. At the beginning of the year, I felt as though I was on top of the world in so many ways, thriving forward and healed from past traumas that I have experienced in my time here on this earth. Or so I thought. And then March came. Seemingly overnight, my life changed. I had always loved working for myself because of the notion that I would never fire myself. Moving into victim mode, as I watched my business and means of income disappear, sunk me further into despair with the belief that life had fired me. As the months went on, I sunk deeper. The days began to run into one another, and it got to a point where I didn't know what week it was. Nor did I care. My triggers had brought my past fears, limiting beliefs, depression, and pain to the surface. Time continued on, and so did my stress along with the stress of everyone around me. I was now at the point where I had nothing to give to anyone. With my energy sucked dry, I found myself in a downward spiral of mental, emotional, and spiritual conflict. What I would do about it was the more pressing question. How much longer could I continue this way before an utter and complete breakdown? Or had that already happened?

She was carefully walking along a bridge above the clouds. As she neared the end, she looked across and spotted another bridge hidden in the hazy night. How far away was the adjacent structure? If she had to guess, it was three feet max. Suddenly, the pavement beneath her feet began to sway. It started off slowly at first, but the longer she teetered, its speed increased. The fear in her gut rose to her throat as she realized that she would either have to remain on the bridge she was on or take a leap of faith onto the other bridge. And there wasn't much time to decide. Could she make it? She was so tired from carrying the baggage down the path and questioned her resolve. "It's just a few feet, you can do it," she promised herself. She threw everything off her back that she was hauling down the stretch and flung herself into the unknown space. Would something, anything be there to catch her?

I've always had vivid dreams. My subconscious speaks to me while I'm asleep. One had been reoccurring in some version for months, and its message was clear to me. "You can't quit. You can't give up." I had begun to find a little motivation to pick myself up out of the darkness that I was swimming in. I dropped my pride and borrowed money from family and friends to get me through the next few months. That, along with a little work trickling in, relieved some of the stress so I could begin to see through the fog I was lost in. One night, after scrolling on social media, I stumbled upon a spiritual life coach. I felt a calling, and although I couldn't afford it, I did it anyway. That proved to be one of the best decisions I've ever made. I was tired, broken, and in need of guidance, unable to see the things in front of me that my deeper self already knew.

It was in this space that I began to heal and clear the blockages that have held me back. It was also here that I became grateful for the opportunity to be still as life unfolded, without the need to control any outcome. This release allowed for things to begin aligning back into much needed balance. We sit here today still uncertain of where things are headed. But do we ever really know? I, for one, have come to a place of love, hope, and trust with the faith that our journeys will continue and that the sky is the limit when we find the strength to overcome any storms we find ourselves in.

Laurie is a creative professional and aspiring author currently working on her first novel. She lives in South Louisiana with her fur baby, Magnolia, and enjoys cooking, reading, journaling, working out, and meditating.

JESS GRAY

THE RUN OF MY LIFE

"Do not go gentle into that good night. Rage, rage against the dying of the light" – Dylan Thomas

In the winter of 2020, I was in a pretty comfortable place. I was working 45-50 hours a week at a stable, legal job, I had just started a comfortable – if not terribly fast-paced relationship – -I had a role in an original and really innovative community theatre piece, and then I woke up and the world had changed.

I am a contagion dork. I've seen the documentaries on SARS more times than I would like to admit. I am a nerd for the science of viral spread and socio-biological impact. This is all to tell you I am very cool, but also that I knew what was coming in about the middle of February, if COVID truly hit the States. Perhaps not the level of candid apathy from some of my fellow countrymen, but given the contingency of novel viruses, I knew we were, well for lack of a better term...fucked.

This knowledge essentially led to the loss of my job because I questioned the firm's safety practices. They said it was because I "mislabeled a letter to a client"...*legally* (I do mean legally, they threatened me with a cease and desist) I have to say that is the reason for termination. Either way I was terminated; so cross off stable, legal job; cross off health insurance; cross off fiscal security.

Then there was my relationship. My boyfriend, though amazing, happened to live with a set of female roommates who were... let's judicially say, jealous. I was being screened twice a week for COVID-19, seeing my primary care physician and immunologist frequently. However, his roommates decided they knew better. When we followed my doctors' advice on how to best begin co-quarantining, after an exceedingly long safety period apart, they rationally responded by breaking a souvenir he had brought back from a vacation with his grandmother. They went so far as to key my car, which felt excessive and dramatic even to me, and I am an actress. So, cross off comfortable relationship. These were two twenty-year-olds with twenty-year-old friends and a lot of time on their hands; so write it on a legal pad and then redact it, we went from stable and cozy to Defcon 5.

My theatre piece got cancelled along with my cousin's graduation, my best friend's wedding, a family vacation, my grandfather's birthday, the County Fair, haunted houses, an aunt's funeral, movie theatres, the Rein Fair, the Fourth of July, Memorial Day, Halloween, and Presidents Day. So cross off joy, excitement, and all bank holidays.

Did I mention I have an autoimmune disorder (thus the many doctors' appointments)? Because of this I was forced to stay mostly indoors, but also because my immune system can be overly aggressive and I was in a mask far more often, I ended up with tonsillitis and an excruciating ear infection (I do not encourage a burst eardrum at 37, it is painful and infantilizing). So, cross off my safety and health as well.

So now comes the turn, right? The part of the essay when I dazzle you with my ability to take the fear and magically turn it into a bouquet of hope...

I am sorry dear reader; I am not that good of a writer.

Bullies are not okay, hate isn't okay, jealousy and property damage are not okay, aggressive and destructive capitalism is not okay, none of this for any of us is okay. It's ugly and dark, it blocks out the sun and any cloud, let alone a silver lining in sight. The world right now is not okay.

But…

About two weeks after getting fired I forced myself to take up running. I had a simple goal: I wanted to run one 5K, (I told myself I would get strong enough to fight back). I am now the proud owner of one 5K medal, one 8K and one 10K medal.

Since I had started running, I told myself it was ridiculous that I was still smoking, it is hard enough to breathe when you are running… So, I quit smoking.

I had the time, so I returned to writing, I wrote a short play and then another, and a slightly longer play and I am proud to say I am now an award-winning playwright.

I took up painting.

I swallowed my fear and ventured back out into the workforce after four months of being safe inside. I found a job I love, with less hours, and a far less abusive atmosphere.

My boyfriend moved out of his toxic apartment, and things with us sped up, we now live together (unless his grandmother is reading this).

There is no silver lining to this pandemic, there is no sunlight shining down on the world right now. People are more ready to destroy each other than ever, companies are more ready to chew their employees up and spit them out, jealousy, greed, anger, and darkness are having their moments covering the sun… you can't look to the sky to find hope when the night is at its darkest. You must crack your ribs open; take out your still beating, brave, little heart; and follow its weak but steady beam into that night. *You* are the silver lining, you have to be your own sunlight, no one is going to put your oxygen mask on for you. Lace up your tennis shoes, and go running. Fix your eyes on the horizon and have faith – if in nothing else, have faith in yourself.

We are all our own tiny miracles just for making it this far. And if the world could change before, *it can* and will change again, and I will be right there next to you running into the sunlight when it does.

Huh, maybe I am that good of a writer.

Jess Gray is a legal professional, award-winning playwright, and an in-house writer and performer for NEON Theatre. She dedicates this work to Tyler, Kaylee and Kyler for always being my sunshine.

Kristina Anderson

Purpose in the Pause

What was this? What was this stealthy, living, breathing, evolving entity that suddenly had the country in its grip? What was this thing that thrust us indoors and abruptly made us decide what and who was 'essential'? What was this thing that ground our lives to a screeching halt? Coronavirus. COVID-19. A virus that forced a nation to quarantine and isolate. To sit inside with your thoughts, good, bad or indifferent. I've heard various names given to this peculiar and alarming time we're living in. The Sacred Pause. The Season of Stillness. The New Normal. This time has also revealed that writers are desperately needed to record the space that we're uncomfortably navigating. This time of COVID-19 is breaking our hearts, but it's also stretching our limits and making us individually and collectively forge mightily ahead to summon the courage and determination to not just survive this time but be aggressively victorious. And those stories need to be written.

To my fellow writers, we must write. It's been difficult and distracting, but it's our charge as the scribes of this world to chronicle the times we are living in. We must truthfully record how wearing masks and social distancing immediately became part of our daily lives. We must truthfully record while this country was being ravaged by a voracious virus, healthcare workers unselfishly put their lives on the line to save the lives of others. We must truthfully record how school systems created plans to feed children who were sent home in the middle of the school year because it was no longer safe in the buildings. We must truthfully record how artists started consoling and entertaining us online to help divert our attention from the weariness of what was happening in our country. We must truthfully record how scientists quickly started researching and working diligently to come up with a solution to the pathogen we were experiencing. We must truthfully record how grocery workers, postal workers, first responders, sanitation workers, call center and warehouse workers and truck drivers continued to work tirelessly to keep our country moving ahead. We must truthfully record how houses of worship showed us you don't need to be in a building to worship, they pivoted and safely served their congregations online. We must truthfully record how millions of people around the world took to the streets in the middle of a world health crisis to protest racial injustice. It is our job as writers to present a record of our resilience during this time. Writing isn't just our art, it's our activism.

So I'm encouraging writers, whether you choose to create an in-depth missive or a message breviloquent in nature, to write the epistles of truth and bequeath that record to future generations, because they will need to see that the year 2020 wasn't a year just mired in COVID and chaos, but a year of the mighty conquest.

A U.S. Marine Corps veteran, wife and mother of two, I've been writing poetry and short stories since the age of 10 and am working on my first book for publication.

VIBHA SUBRAMANIAM

LOKA

"Loka Samastha Sukhino Bhavantu" is the prayer that
comes to my mind every night when I go to bed. In Sanskrit
this simply means, "May the world live in happiness". I
remember hearing about the coronavirus early this year,
and was oblivious of the impact it was going to have on
every one of us – and when I say every one of us, I literally
mean the 7.7 billion+ people leaving on Planet Earth. There
was a lot of cynicism and skepticism in the air. People at
my yoga studio said, "Not sure what the fuss is about, more
than 10,000 people die of the flu in the US every year. This is
so over-hyped". I was not sure if I should jump on the same
band-wagon or not ,from all that we were hearing about the
effects this virus had on fellow human beings in Wuhan. From
life being normal one day, everything changed overnight. To
being offered the choice of working from home, to having
to mandatorily work from home, the kids' school shutting
down, all four of us were now at home, with a lot of fear in
every one's minds. With time passing, all of us have adapted
to the 'new normal', kids having online classes, and for us to
be working from home.

Images from India of the tens of thousands of migrant
workers walking many miles to go home, holding onto all
their belongings, with despair in their eyes. Similar images
started emerging from within the United States, with long
lines of people waiting at food banks, overcrowded hospitals.
These images haunt me every day. That's when I truly

understood the meaning of the phrase 'Count your Blessings'. While there have been a lot of minor inconveniences, by and large, we cannot complain since we have a roof over our head, both my spouse and I still have our jobs, there is food on the table.

This pandemic has made us critically aware of how some people still don't trust science, and are so selfish that they can only think about the fun they need to have, while there are fellow human beings who are dying in this country. All they are asking us to do is to stay put at home, wear masks, avoid large crowds. In comparison to the sacrifices that they are making, that is the least we can do on our part to not overwhelm the hospital system.

However, it has also brought out the best in all of us. We have learned to be more compassionate, and have put things in perspective. It has taught us that the most important thing in life is life itself, and that we must truly be grateful to be alive. It has taught us not to take anything or anyone for granted, and to respect all the essential workers, who put their lives in harm's way, just to keep us safe.

I have been in touch with friends, who I know are living by themselves, with no shoulder to lean on, no support system like I have. It is hard for people who are alone; they can drift into depression because of the current circumstances. Staying connected with family and friends who are alone lets them know that they are not alone in this, and that they can reach out to me anytime they need someone to talk to. This not only helps our friends, but also puts things in perspective for us.

Personally for me, this pandemic has also taught me to slow down, to spend more time with the children, to re-discover old recipes passed down by generations in our family, to focus on my health, on things I like to do as a person, get some quality time with my daughter who will be off to college next year, help the family navigate these unprecedented times, and to keep praying for this pandemic to pass. We are a resilient species, and we will conquer this just as we have done with recovering from World Wars, pandemics, 9/11.

Each of us have a way of dealing with this crisis, and for me, keeping calm, taking one day at a time, and ever being grateful for each day that is bestowed upon us has helped me steer through the madness we are in. Stay safe. Stay calm, and remember, this too shall pass. I shall end the way I began "Loka Samastha Sukhino Bhavantu". Peace and Happiness to one and all!

Vibha Subramaniam is a wife and mother of two amazing kids! IT Professional in the Bay Area, loves hiking, hanging out with friends, cooking. Motto in life is to "Keep Calm and Carry On"!

RICHARD CAREY

HOME, FINALLY

It's dark, air filled with crickets and a distant barking dog. A fog's come in, I can smell it: salty and light. The gravel driveway crunches as the usual sounds of my homecoming welcome me: the three *thunks* of a stubborn door knob, a whispered creak from my screen door, and the light flick of a lamp.

My bed's not made, but I never do that anyway, the stained comforter flung neatly across my college apartment bed sheets. I make a mental note to buy new ones.

I remember I brewed coffee for the next morning and I thank my coffee machine – a gift from my grandmother two Christmases ago – for the many broken mornings mended. I look around my studio, thankful I cleaned before: bare counters and clean dishes. I heel my shoes off and put my bags down, turn on the bathroom faucet and soap up. The new routine of a new age. A new home. The space hums with me.

Back in March, as the world tipped over a sudden ledge, I was serving at local restaurants in rural Virginia. After a failed attempt at securing a full-time position in San Francisco the summer before, I decided to reset and use the house where my mother and siblings lived as the temporary solution to my lack of career prospects.

Winter never really came and spring kissed our doors. Instead of feeling excited to start a new journey, dread filled

284

the corners of my head as the tolls of the pandemic's victims climbed. I already felt I missed the train of opportunity so many of my peers hopped on soon after graduation. I was already reeling from the pressures of careers and post-graduate life and the expectations I set for myself. What do you do when you're already in freefall and the world still rips the carpet from under your feet?

A heaviness rested on my shoulders. A heaviness rested on the world's shoulders. The spaces I lived in during the last four years were always temporary. Planting roots meant locking down and remaining. I was scared of complacency. I always prolonged living in a suitcase by chance I'd need to pack quickly for an unread job offer in my inbox that never came.

I succumbed to the defeat of finding myself in the epicenter of the self-loathing still squatting in my bones since elementary school. Permanence eyed me from its corner, knowing all inclinations my stay in rural Virginia to be brief would also be false.

Stay-at-home orders were enacted and I hadn't felt at home in years. I felt like a visitor in the house I was forced to quarantine.

I needed to evolve, listening to when my body was ready and taking the mornings slow. Reading with breakfast before turning to a screen. Some yard work or exercise with the dogs. Coffee until lunch. Something light before a workout that becomes a habit now lost. I become more patient with my family. We're in a pandemic – stress clouds the eves of every home in America. A different fog.

We tilled the garden with manure. *It's going to be a good one.* I began to admire the late evenings when the air turned gray and I'd notice the grass too long and promise – for myself – to my brother *I'll mow tomorrow.*

And I would because days needed to be filled. I'd curtain off an alcove to be alone, able to indulge in the orange sky at seven thirty. I'd watered our plants and buy a tree for Mother's Day. Another plant to hang on the porch she stands on during thunderstorms.

Corners were swept from cobwebs and anxiety. I watched the statistics climb and acknowledged how lucky I was. How privileged I am. My path hadn't crossed with the pandemic's and I was able to stay hidden. I had a roof and family, a refrigerator with leftovers. I had a home to quarantine under.

I felt secured. I smiled at the walls and closed cabinets carefully. I liked to guess if it was cloudy through my blackout curtains. I was always wrong.

My mom would always make sure to ask if anybody needed anything specific before our semi-weekly grocery run. A special request was rare but justified. My favorite creamer became a crutch, any snack with a crunch welcomed, sweet treats as medicine. Mom never really needed anything, so I'd cook dinner for the family and clean after. I think she appreciated it.

I cook for myself now and still appreciate it, but a bit less. I clean the dishes to less enjoyment and have suddenly been tethered to a seven o'clock wake up. But I still love the quiet mornings. I'll open my door and let the leaves whisper through my screen. I'll make a coffee with the same creamer and eat slowly in bed.

I'll work and be thankful for a job, come home to the comforting sounds and begin again. I sometimes enjoy the long way to work as I pass the ocean in the morning and promise to visit soon. And I will because the days still need to be filled.

I'll remember the orange light from my alcove window and think how different the pink sky here reflects off the waves. It's quieter without my family. I let the studio breathe on its own. Sometimes I never want to leave.

I grew up in rural Virginian suburbia decorated with DO NOT LITTER and Confederate Flags. I knew I was a faggot before I knew I was gay. I considered it the last place to be home for a long time.

I call my mom twice during the week. She always asks if I need anything. I always answer no.

I was born in Boston, MA and grew up in rural Virginia. In 2019, I graduated from James Madison University with a degree in Communications. I currently live on Nantucket, Massachusetts where I enjoy the trails behind my apartment and quiet mornings in town.

Luke W. Henderson

"New Normal" Isn't Normal, and Normal Was Never Normal

I remember the start of the pandemic; everyone was boundlessly optimistic even with the successive closings of schools and businesses. We would all stay home, we would 'flatten the curve'. Sure, the isolation and mundaneness would be hard, but it would be worth it and to many, an opportunity. Spouses were making music together, others picking up old hobbies, and many were catching up with old friends.

Unfortunately, this was not my experience.

I was an extreme utilizer of the gig economy. After thirty thousand dollars in student loans, like many in my generation, I was having difficulty finding well-paying, relevant employment. So, I took whatever small jobs I could, from being an usher at the St. Louis Symphony, a substitute teacher, and a summertime truck driver when the other jobs were out. To add to this load, I had a graduate degree to finally break this cycle of gigs. This was my normal. It gave me the flexibility and options for income.

It all came down like a rockslide when quarantine started.

First, the symphony canceled concerts, and shortly after the schools closed. I was like everyone else, boundlessly optimistic, so I figured the quick fix would be my truck driving gig. My optimism was upturned when they said they couldn't find work for me, being affected like everyone else.

Dread immediately filled my mind. It was unclear whether I qualified for unemployment, as substituting was a staffing job and the symphony technically didn't furlough me.

I started asking around for jobs and applied to places, but I was initially unsuccessful. Even my previous experience and education couldn't get me interviews at places that were supposedly in high demand of employees. Desperately, I quickly wrote some music for people to buy and help out which only yielded $45. My future looked fairly grim. Thankfully, my truck driving gig found a way to bring me back.

I didn't have pandemic-friendly work, having to touch people's furniture and often had nearby mask-free groups on porches. In fact, some customers complained that our masks made them uncomfortable because it made us look sick. The work wasn't consistent, but my family and I managed.

This was my 'new' normal.

It was at this point I began questioning whether this 'new' normal was real, or if 'normal' ever existed.

Now it's August and things are semi-consistent, but it doesn't feel like normal. But really, what is normal about *being*? Outside of maybe the ultra-wealthy, there's no point where a person can claim that their life isn't changing. We're constantly making goals and then new goals. There are marriages, babies, breakups, deaths, along with a million other things from year-to-year. Which of these points is normal?

Even our bodies are constantly changing. The different types of cells in our bodies are constantly dying and being replaced at different intervals. Throughout our lives, we acquire injuries, fluctuate in weight, and health. When are our bodies normal?

This pandemic shows that we don't truly experience normal. What is normal is what we deem acceptable changes.

We expect weight loss and changing relationships, but these typically don't have the drastic effect COVID-19 has had on the world. Coronavirus was quick and uncontrollable and suddenly it was global and governments declared lockdowns. Decisions were swift and without democracy, which made many uncomfortable even if they agreed in principle. People experienced the scientific process in real-time, which came across as a contradiction.

Society was so used to a normal where changes had solutions, or at a minimum a wealth of guidance. This idea is so ingrained and worshipped that large changes completely rock our world. COVID-19 destroyed the pedestal of normality. It was unprecedented with no easy references on survival, control, or management.

The pandemic made me feel helpless and it was worse because my life wasn't upended by something I could easily blame, but by nature – a faceless, uncaring entity. COVID-19 was like the creatures in *Birdbox* or *A Quiet Place*. Those creatures are so effective in scaring the audience due to a lack of information, a lack of motive. We find comfort in bad when there are reasons behind it. This is why we don't consider Lex Luthor or the Joker to be horror icons. When there is no rationality behind the monsters, the uncertainty is more terrifying than the monsters themselves.

I was shown that my normal had always been teetering on a cliff, tied down with content because there was a past I could draw from. Now, I'm not so convinced it ever existed. 'New normal' suggests a motion from point A to point B, but that's not the case. 'New normal' has felt like a rabbit trying to evade a predator through erratic zigs and zags with no clear ending. In a way, there never will be an ending, for it will be generations before there are children with no connection to the COVID-19 pandemic. When in the future will anything be normal again?

Simply put, it won't, and there's no telling when 'new normal' will crumble.

I hope people start viewing their own lives through this lens.

This nostalgic optimism clouds our ambition and prevents us from truly seeing life's full picture. It's not a constant nihilistic trance, floating unstably through life, but an inkling that this could all be taken away. It's not dread, but an appreciation that we have anything right now, and it's never normal. Normal is a tool, not a doctrine, and regarding it as such does little good.

Whenever 'post-COVID' finally arrives, I'll know to love what I have at this moment and change what I can. I'll know that yearning for a return to normal or accepting a 'new normal' is silly because neither really exists. I'll recognize that life is constantly changing and I cannot be prepared for everything, so instead, I'll ride the wave and take the winds instead of capsizing. I will be free of the confines of a normal and seek truth over comfort.

Luke W. Henderson is a writer pretending to be a full-time truck driver. He is a contributing author to Igniting Liberty: Voices For Freedom From Around The World *as well as multiple websites. Luke also composes music for fine art, and electronic mediums as well as film.*

Made in the USA
Monee, IL
30 May 2021